Fish

GENERAL EDITOR
CHUCK WILLIAMS

RECIPES
JOYCE GOLDSTEIN

PHOTOGRAPHY
ALLAN ROSENBERG

TIME
LIFE
BOOKS

TIME-LIFE BOOKS
Time-Life Books is a division of Time Life Inc.
Time-Life is a trademark of Time Warner Inc. U.S.A.

Time-Life Custom Publishing
Vice President and Publisher: Terry Newell
Vice President of Sales and Marketing: Neil Levin
Director of Financial Operations: J. Brian Birky
Director of Acquisitions: Jennifer L. Pearce

WILLIAMS-SONOMA
Founder and Vice Chairman: Chuck Williams
Associate Book Buyer: Cecilia Michaelis

WELDON OWEN INC.
President: John Owen
Vice President and Publisher: Wendely Harvey
Chief Operating Officer: Larry Partington
Vice President International Sales: Stuart Laurence
Managing Editor: Laurie Wertz
Consulting Editor: Norman Kolpas
Copy Editor: Sharon Silva
Design/Editorial Assistant: Janique Poncelet
Design: John Bull, The Book Design Company
Production: Stephanie Sherman, James Obata,
   Mick Bagnato
Production Coordinator: Tarji Mickelson
Food Photographer: Allan Rosenberg
Additional Food Photography: Allen V. Lott
Primary Food & Prop Stylist: Sandra Griswold
Food Stylist: Heidi Gintner
Assistant Food Stylist: Danielle Di Salvo
Glossary Illustrations: Alice Harth

The Williams-Sonoma Kitchen Library
conceived and produced by Weldon Owen Inc.
814 Montgomery St., San Francisco, CA 94133

In collaboration with Williams-Sonoma
3250 Van Ness Ave., San Francisco, CA 94109

Printed in China by Toppan Printing Co., LTD.

A Note on Weights and Measures:
All recipes include customary U.S. and metric measurements. Metric conversions are based on a standard developed for these books and have been rounded off. Actual weights may vary.

A Weldon Owen Production
Copyright © 1993 Weldon Owen Inc.
Reprinted in 1994; 1994; 1994; 1995; 1996; 1997;
   1998; 1998; 1999; 2000

Library of Congress
Cataloging-in-Publication Data:

Goldstein, Joyce Esersky.
   Fish / general editor, Chuck Williams ;
recipes, Joyce Goldstein ; photography,
Allan Rosenberg.
      p.   cm. — (Williams-Sonoma kitchen library)
   Includes index.
   ISBN 0-7835-0262-1 (trade) ;
   ISBN 0-7835-0263-X (lib. bdg.)
   1. Cookery (Fish)   I. Williams, Chuck.
II. Title.   III. Series.
TX747.G59   1994
641.6'92—dc20   93-28238
                                       CIP

Contents

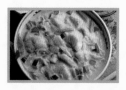

BRAISED, POACHED & STEAMED 17

SAUTÉED & FRIED 35

BROILED & GRILLED 55

BAKED & ROASTED 73

SALADS 97

INTRODUCTION

In recent years, we've witnessed nothing less than a revolution in the way cooks everywhere think about fish. Not so long ago, canned tuna or battered and fried cod summed up the average person's seafood intake—except for the occasional evening out to dine on fillet of sole at some elegant restaurant. Fish was seldom on the dining table more than once a week, if that often.

But not anymore. Today, tuned into the health benefits eating fish can bring, we're enjoying it every day of the week. And even those of us who live hundreds of miles from coastal waters are dipping into—thanks to modern air freight—an ocean bounty of huge dimensions. Salmon, halibut, sturgeon, sea bass, shark, snapper, turbot: All these fish and more appear on restaurant menus and on home tables everywhere, cooked and seasoned in myriad ways. Even lifelong meat eaters are discovering the delicious flavors of grilled swordfish and *fresh* tuna.

This book recognizes the new esteem we feel for fish in all its variety. It begins with a survey of kitchen equipment for preparing all kinds of fish with maximum ease, followed by basic guidelines for selecting and cooking any kind of fish to perfection. The 44 recipes from around the world, each accompanied by a full-color photograph, are organized by cooking method: braised, poached and steamed fish; sautéed and fried; broiled and grilled; baked and roasted; and fish salads.

Whichever recipe you choose to make, I'd like to add two important pieces of advice. First, always seek out the freshest fish; ask around to find the most reputable fishmonger near you and never settle for less than the best quality. Second, always take care not to overcook fish; follow closely the guidelines on pages 8–10 and in the individual recipes.

I'm sure you'll be impressed by how quick, easy and delicious—and good for you—fish can be.

EQUIPMENT

All-purpose and specialized tools treat fresh, high-quality fish with the utmost culinary respect

You needn't go on a shopping expedition for special equipment to be able to prepare a wide variety of fish dishes. Good-quality, all-purpose pots, pans and baking dishes will meet the needs of most recipes in this book.

But a few pieces of specialized equipment will make the simple task of cooking fish easier still. A fish spatula, for example, has a curved and elongated shape that helps keep whole fish or fillets from falling apart when you turn them on the grill. A fish poacher, tailored to the shape of most whole fish or large fillets, allows for easier cooking and spectacular presentations. Parchment paper, cheesecloth, skewers, a double boiler and a deep-frying thermometer can each in its own small way add extra finesse to your fish-cooking skills.

1. Stockpot
Tall, deep, large-capacity pot with close-fitting lid, for making stock or fish stews. Select a good-quality, heavy pot that absorbs and transfers heat well.

2. Mixing Bowls
Sturdy bowls in a range of sizes for all-purpose use, from straining stock to marinating fish to mixing seafood salads. Made of earthenware, porcelain, glass or stainless steel.

3. Spatula
Sturdy, rectangular-bladed spatula for all-purpose use when grilling, sautéing or panfrying fish.

4. Skimmer
Wide bowl and fine mesh for efficient removal of froth and scum from surface of fish stock and for removing deep-fried fish from hot oil.

5. Fish Spatula
Concave, horizontal blade facilitates neat turning of small to medium-sized whole fish or fish fillets during grilling or sautéing.

6. Double Boiler
For preparing hollandaise sauce, a classic fish accompaniment. The sauce cooks in the upper pan over the gentle steam heat created by water simmering in the lower pan.

7. Assorted Kitchen Tools

Wire whisks for blending liquid ingredients and stirring sauces; wooden and metal spoons for all-purpose mixing and stirring; brushes for basting and glazing; ladle for serving fish soups and stews; deep-frying thermometer for accurately measuring cooking temperature of hot oil.

8. Fish Poacher

Long, deep, heavy-duty pan holds whole fish or large fillets for poaching in hot liquid.

9. Skewers

For holding together small pieces of fish during grilling or broiling; wooden or bamboo skewers may also be used to secure stuffed and rolled fish fillets. Before using, soak wooden and bamboo skewers in water for 30 minutes to prevent burning.

10. Baking Dishes

Select heavy-duty glazed porcelain, stoneware, earthenware or glass for oven-baked fish recipes.

11. Cheesecloth

For straining fine particles from fish stock. Also for wrapping fish for poaching to facilitate lowering it into and removing it from the cooking liquid. Muslin may also be used.

12. Sauté Pan

Select a well-made heavy metal pan large enough to hold pieces of fish in a single layer without crowding when sautéing. Straight sides help contain splattering. Close-fitting lid covers pan for moist cooking.

13. Saucepan

For simmering stock and sauces and for cooking small fish stews and braises.

14. Steamer Basket

Petaled, flowerlike shape enables the basket to expand or contract to fit saucepans of various sizes, to hold food above the level of simmering liquid. Small center post is used to lift the basket out of the pan once food is cooked.

15. Kitchen Knives

For general ingredient preparation and for slicing and serving cooked fish. Long, slender blade of smaller knife is also useful for boning fish fillets.

16. Parchment Paper

Sturdy, heatproof, stick-resistant paper can be used to wrap fish for oven baking *en papillote*—"in an envelope."

17. Food Processor

For general chopping, slicing and puréeing of ingredients, particularly in large quantities.

18. Frying Pan

Choose good-quality, heavy stainless steel, thick aluminum, cast iron or heavy enameled steel for rapid browning or frying. Flared sides facilitate turning and allow moisture to escape easily for more crisp results.

19. Mortar and Pestle

For crushing garlic or other seasonings.

A GUIDE TO FISH

Easy-to-follow tips for seeking out, selecting, storing and cooking the best-quality fish for any recipe

For the ease and speed that today's cooks demand, most of the recipes in this collection use fresh fish fillets—that is, boneless portions of fish. A few, for the sake of authenticity or for an impressive presentation, are based on fish steaks or whole fish.

For the most part, the terms used for fish in this book describe categories rather than specific types of fish. Sometimes recipes specify "white fish," which refers to the color of the flesh of the fish. Also, freshwater fish, such as catfish, trout and carp, are prepared essentially the same way as their saltwater cousins within the same category. The aim is to make the recipes as versatile as possible, allowing you the option of buying whatever fish is freshest and most reasonably priced in the market. To help you make your selection, the following broad categories apply to the recipes in this book; they principally encompass the most common U.S. varieties:

Firm, Lean Fish. Generally low-fat varieties with mild to delicate flavor and firm flesh that, when cooked, forms visible layers, or "flakes," that separate easily. Such flakes may be fine or coarse. Includes bass, cod, flounder, grouper, haddock, halibut, some mullet varieties, perch, pike, rockfish, sea bass, skate (ray), snapper, sole and turbot. Salmon and trout will also flake, although they are less lean and possess distinctive though not strong flavors. All these fish are suited to a wide range of cooking methods.

Meaty Fish. Ranging in fat content from low to high and with a correspondingly diverse range of flavors and textures, these fish are usually cut in thick steaks or fillets for broiling, grilling or baking; they may also successfully be poached, steamed, sautéed or braised. Includes catfish, eel, monkfish (anglerfish), northern halibut, orange roughy, shark, sturgeon, swordfish and some tuna varieties.

Fatty or strong-flavored fish. Varieties whose high fat content produces a pronounced flavor. Includes bluefish, butterfish, carp, herring, mackerel, some mullet varieties, shad, sardine and some tuna varieties. Best suited to baking, broiling or grilling with a strong-flavored sauce that stands up well to the fish.

SELECTING THE FRESHEST FISH

The growing popularity of fish and the common use of air freight make a wide variety of fresh fish available most everywhere, even in locations far from oceans, lakes or rivers. Still, it is worth the effort to search your neighborhood for the best fish source you can find. Look for a market with the most varied selection, with a frequent turnover ensuring the freshest product, and with a level of personal service that allows you to special-order specific varieties or cuts of fish.

When making your selection, keep a few simple guidelines in mind. Above all, do not buy any fish that actually smells fishy, indicating that it is no longer fresh or hasn't been cut or stored properly. Fresh fish has the mild, clean scent of the sea—nothing more. Fish fillets or steaks should look bright, lustrous and moist, with no signs of discoloration or drying. Whole fish will have bright, shiny, well-attached scales; bright pink or red gills; firm, elastic flesh that springs back to the touch; and eyes that are bright, clear and full, never clouded or sunken.

Sometimes only so-called fresh-frozen fish fillets or steaks will be available—that is, fish that was frozen on board ship, soon after it was caught. Buy them still frozen, if possible, making sure they appear undamaged and free of discoloration or dry-looking freezer burn; defrost the fish lightly covered in a shallow dish in your refrigerator before cooking. If the fish has already been defrosted by the fishmonger, apply to it the same criteria of smell, sight and touch you would to fresh fish. Be sure to ask how long it has been defrosted, shunning anything thawed for more than 2 days. Never refreeze fish that has already been defrosted.

Storing Fish at Home

Always aim to cook fresh or defrosted frozen fish within 24 hours of its purchase. Until you cook it, remove the store wrapping and rewrap the fish in plastic wrap or aluminum foil. Keep it in the coldest part of your refrigerator.

Frozen fish should be stored wrapped in heavy foil or in moistureproof or vaporproof freezer paper, at a temperature no higher than 0°F (-20°C). Cook it within 2 months of purchase, and preferably sooner.

Smoked and Canned Fish

Some recipes in this book call for popular varieties of fish preserved by smoking or canning. The following guidelines will assist you in your selection:

Smoked salmon. Purchase smoked salmon freshly sliced from a good-quality delicatessen. Lox, which is a salt-cured salmon, and Nova, which is a cold-smoked salmon, are commonly sold in Jewish delicatessens; they have oilier textures and in most cases are not acceptable substitutes for smoked salmon.

Smoked trout. Sold in specialty-food stores and delicatessens, either in fillets or as whole fish requiring skinning and boning, smoked trout has a mild, sweet flavor and moist, tender texture. Look for smoked trout that appears moist and firm; avoid a dry-looking product.

Canned anchovy. The tiny saltwater fish, related to sardines, are preserved in cans in salt or oil. Imported anchovy fillets packed in olive oil are the most commonly available. Anchovies packed in salt, available in some Italian delicatessens, are considered the finest; rinse and fillet before use.

Canned tuna. If possible, buy the best-quality, solid-pack albacore tuna, canned in olive oil. The finest brands are imported from Italy, available in Italian delicatessens and quality food stores. For a lower-fat product, search out water-packed albacore tuna.

Preparing Fish for Cooking

When you're ready to cook a piece of fish, trim any rough edges to assure a neater look. If you wish, or if the recipe calls for it, use a small, sharp knife to cut away the skin from fillets or steaks, or ask your fishmonger to do this for you. (If you are purchasing a whole fish, ask your fishmonger to gut and scale the fish and to trim off the fins and gills.) Check fillets along their edges and ribcage line to make sure that all small bones have been removed. If any small bones poke out, grasp them firmly with your fingers and remove by pulling in the direction they're pointing. If necessary, use kitchen tweezers or small pliers.

BASIC COOKING INSTRUCTIONS

While every recipe in this book provides specific cooking times and instructions, the following guidelines offer help in cooking any type of fish in any recipe.

Baking fish fillets. Preheat the oven to 450°F (230°C). Sprinkle the fish with salt and pepper and place in an oiled baking dish. Bake 8–10 minutes for a 6-ounce (185-g) fillet, depending upon its thickness.

Broiling or grilling fish fillets. Preheat a broiler (griller) or prepare a charcoal fire. Brush the fish lightly with olive oil or clarified butter and sprinkle with salt and pepper. Broil or grill, turning once, 3–4 minutes on each side for a 6-ounce (185-g) fillet, depending upon its thickness.

Poaching fish fillets. In a wide, deep sauté pan with high sides, pour in poaching liquid, such as court bouillon or water, to a depth of 2 inches (5 cm). Bring to a boil and lower the heat to a bare simmer. Slip in the fillets, cover and poach for 6–8 minutes for a 6-ounce (185-g) fillet, depending upon its thickness. (You may also poach fish uncovered, but you'll need a greater depth of poaching liquid as it will steam away more quickly.) Remove the fish and blot it dry. To prepare an accompanying sauce, boil the poaching liquid until it reduces in volume and intensifies in flavor, then beat in cream or butter and seasonings of your choice.

Baking a whole fish. Preheat an oven to 450°F (230°C). Place the fish in an oiled baking dish. Bake for 8–10 minutes per 1 inch (2.5 cm) of thickness measured at the fish's thickest point, basting occasionally.

Poaching a whole fish. In a poaching pan large enough to hold the fish comfortably, bring to a boil enough poaching liquid to submerge the fish completely. Lower the heat to a bare simmer and slip in the fish. Cover and poach for 10 minutes per 1 inch (2.5 cm) of thickness measured at the fish's thickest point.

Broiling or grilling a whole fish. Preheat the broiler (griller) or prepare a charcoal fire. Brush the fish lightly with olive oil or clarified butter and sprinkle with salt and pepper. Broil or grill for about 8 minutes per 1 inch (2.5 cm) of thickness measured at the fish's thickest point.

TESTING FISH FOR DONENESS

Following the cooking time guidelines above will help you achieve perfectly cooked fish in any recipe. But because fish cooks quickly and tends to dry out when overcooked, it's a good idea to check fish at the earliest moment it may be done to ensure results that are always moist and tender.

For fillets or steaks, use a small knife to make a slit in the fish (right). For whole fish, you could also insert a metal skewer into the thickest part of the fish and then touch it to your tongue; it should feel hot.

Cutting a slit
When a fish fillet has cooked for the minimum time called for in the recipe, use the tip of a small, sharp knife to cut a slit into the thickest part. If the fish is cooked through, it will appear opaque at its center.

Fish Stock

Called fumet in France, this basic fish stock is a good base for fish soups and stews. Pieces of fish can replace part or all of the fish frames, but the flavor of the stock will not be as full-bodied. If you lack time to make stock, bottled clam juice can be used. It is generally quite salty, however, and should be diluted with chicken or vegetable stock when used in large quantities in recipes. The salt in the recipe may need to be reduced as well. Fish stock keeps for 2 days in the refrigerator, or can be frozen for up to 3 months. To make court bouillon, which can be used for poaching fish, omit the fish frames and simmer for only 20 minutes, then strain and refrigerate as directed.

3–4 lb (1.5–2 kg) fish frames (skeletons), including
    heads and tails but with gills removed, from mild-
    flavored fish such as snapper, halibut, flounder or
    rockfish
3 cups (24 fl oz/750 ml) dry white wine
2 yellow onions, coarsely chopped (about 2 cups/
    8 oz/250 g)
2 celery stalks, chopped
2 long strips lemon zest
3 fresh flat-leaf (Italian) parsley sprigs
1 fresh thyme sprig
5 peppercorns
2 coriander seeds
½ bay leaf
5–6 cups (40–48 fl oz/1.25–1.5 l) water, or to cover

*R*inse the fish frames well. Place in a stockpot along with all the remaining ingredients, adding enough water to cover. Bring to a boil over low heat, skimming any scum that rises to the top. Simmer uncovered, skimming occasionally, for about 30 minutes.

Line a colander with cheesecloth (muslin) and strain the stock through it. Refrigerate uncovered, then cover when cold.

Makes about 2 qt (2 l)

Teriyaki Sauce

To save time, prepare a large batch of this traditional Japanese sauce, to have on hand for a quick and simple main dish of grilled or broiled fish. It is especially good on salmon, tuna, trout or mackerel and will keep for a year or so on the pantry shelf. Teriyaki sauce should be at room temperature or warmed slightly before using. Brush the sauce on the fish a few times as it cooks to give it a glazed crust, and then spoon a little more on after cooking. To flavor the sauce with ginger or with citrus zest, add 2 tablespoons grated fresh ginger or 4 teaspoons grated lemon or orange zest for each 1 cup (8 fl oz/250 ml) sauce to be used; bring to a simmer. Remove from the heat and allow to steep for 2 hours before using.

1 cup (8 fl oz/250 ml) mirin
1 cup (8 fl oz/250 ml) sake
1½ cups (12 fl oz/375 ml) soy sauce
½ cup (4 oz/125 g) sugar
¼ cup (2 fl oz/60 ml) light corn syrup

*B*ecause this sauce bubbles up quite high, combine the mirin, sake, soy sauce, sugar and corn syrup in a deep saucepan. Bring to a boil, reduce the heat to medium and simmer until thick, about 30 minutes.

Remove from the heat and let cool.

Makes about 3 cups (24 fl oz/750 ml), enough for 16–20 6-oz (185-g) fish servings

Hollandaise Sauce

Rich and delicious, this sauce is excellent served on simple poached or broiled salmon, trout or halibut when a special occasion calls for gilding the gilled ones. You can make it more quickly by using warm melted clarified butter in place of the chilled butter, whisking it into the egg yolk–water mixture a bit at a time until the sauce thickens. Or, to make a lighter-tasting, thinner sauce, reduce 1 cup (8 fl oz/250 ml) fish stock to ⅓ cup (3 fl oz/80 ml) over high heat, let it cool and then combine it with egg yolks in place of the water.

3 egg yolks
1 tablespoon water
¾–1 cup (6–8 oz/185–250 g) unsalted butter, chilled,
   cut into small cubes
2 tablespoons fresh lemon juice
salt
pinch of cayenne pepper, or to taste

*I*n the top pan of a double boiler over hot water, whisk together the egg yolks and water until foamy and warm. Add the butter cubes, a few at a time, whisking them in until incorporated and the mixture is smooth before adding more butter. Continue adding butter until the sauce is thick, smooth and heavily coats the back of a spoon. Whisk in the lemon juice. Season to taste with salt and cayenne pepper. Serve at once, or keep warm over hot water for up to 2 hours.

Makes about 1 cup (8 fl oz/250 ml), enough for 4 servings

Aïoli

This garlic-laced mayonnaise is good on broiled, grilled, fried or poached fish, or spooned into fish soups. Salmon, halibut and swordfish mate particularly well with it. To flavor the aïoli, add to 1 cup any one of the following: 2 tablespoons grated fresh orange or lemon zest; ½ cup (2 oz/60 g) chopped toasted almonds or walnuts; ½ cup (¾ oz/20 g) chopped fresh basil or mint; 1 red bell pepper (capsicum), roasted, seeded, deribbed and puréed; or 2–3 tablespoons grated fresh ginger. Aïoli can be made 4–6 hours ahead of serving, covered and refrigerated.

1 tablespoon finely minced garlic
1 teaspoon kosher salt, plus salt to taste
2 egg yolks, at room temperature
1 tablespoon fresh lemon juice, or more to taste
2 cups (16 fl oz/500 ml) mild-flavored olive oil
freshly ground pepper

*I*n a mortar with a pestle, grind the garlic and salt until the garlic forms a fine purée. Set aside.

Place the egg yolks and lemon juice in the container of a food processor fitted with the metal blade or in a blender. Pulse once to combine. With the motor running, gradually add the olive oil, a few drops at a time, processing until a mayonnaiselike sauce forms. Once the sauce thickens, the oil may be added in a very fine, slow stream. If the sauce becomes too thick, thin with a little cold water.

Beat in the garlic purée and season to taste with salt and pepper.

Makes about 2 cups (16 fl oz/500 ml)

Hollandaise
Sauce

Aïoli

Tarragon-Shallot Butter

Spread a heaping spoonful of this flavorful butter atop hot grilled fish such as trout, salmon or sea bass. Tarragon goes well with carrots, green beans, beets and asparagus, so keep these vegetables in mind as accompaniments for the fish. Any unused butter may be frozen for up to 3 months.

2 tablespoons unsalted butter, plus 6 tablespoons
   (3 oz/90 g) unsalted butter, at room temperature
¼ cup (1½ oz/45 g) finely minced shallot
½ cup (4 fl oz/125 ml) dry white wine
2 tablespoons chopped fresh tarragon
salt and freshly ground pepper

*I*n a small sauté pan, melt the 2 tablespoons butter over medium heat. Add the shallot and sauté until almost tender, about 3 minutes. Add the wine and cook until the liquid is almost completely absorbed and the mixture is syrupy, 5–7 minutes. Let cool.

   In a small food processor fitted with the metal blade or in a blender, combine the cooled shallot mixture, tarragon and the 6 tablespoons (3 oz/90 g) butter. Pulse to combine; do not overprocess or the texture of the shallot will be lost. Alternatively, combine the ingredients in a bowl and beat together by hand using a whisk or spoon. Season to taste with salt and pepper.

   If not using immediately, pack into a small bowl, cover well and refrigerate. Bring to room temperature before serving.

Makes a rounded ½ cup
(4 oz/125 g), enough for
4 servings

Ginger-Lime Butter

An ideal butter to complement salmon, trout, swordfish, flounder, cod or tuna. The shallot may be omitted, but the sauce will have a sharper taste and be thinner. Store any unused butter in the freezer for up to 3 months.

2 tablespoons unsalted butter, plus 6 tablespoons
   (3 oz/90 g) unsalted butter, at room temperature
2 tablespoons finely minced shallot
6 tablespoons (3 fl oz/80 ml) dry white wine
3 tablespoons grated fresh ginger
2 tablespoons fresh lime juice
1 tablespoon grated lime zest
salt and freshly ground pepper

*I*n a small sauté pan over medium heat, melt the 2 tablespoons butter. Add the shallot and cook until almost tender, about 5 minutes. Add the wine and cook until the liquid is almost completely absorbed and the mixture is syrupy, 5–7 minutes. Let cool.

   In a small food processor fitted with the metal blade or in a blender, combine the cooled shallot mixture, wine, ginger, lime juice and zest and the 6 tablespoons (3 oz/90 g) butter. Pulse to combine; do not overprocess or the texture of the seasonings will be lost. Alternatively, combine the ingredients in a bowl and beat together by hand using a whisk or spoon. Season to taste with salt and pepper.

   If not using immediately, pack into a small bowl, cover well and refrigerate. Bring to room temperature before serving.

Makes a rounded ½ cup (4 oz/125 g), enough for 4 servings

Tarragon-Shallot Butter

Ginger-Lime Butter

Tartar Sauce

The classic American seafood house accompaniment for deep-fried fish (recipe on page 39). Tartar sauce, a well-seasoned mayonnaise, is a variation on the French rémoulade sauce and can also be served with sautéed or broiled fish fillets. For a low-fat alternative, replace half the mayonnaise with plain nonfat or low-fat yogurt.

1 cup (8 fl oz/250 ml) mayonnaise
1 tablespoon Dijon mustard
3 tablespoons finely minced white or yellow onion
2 tablespoons finely minced cornichon
2 tablespoons vinegar from cornichons or distilled white vinegar
1 tablespoon finely chopped, well-drained capers
1 tablespoon finely minced fresh flat-leaf (Italian) parsley
1 tablespoon finely minced fresh chives
½ teaspoon freshly ground pepper
salt

Combine all of the ingredients in a bowl, including salt to taste. Whisk to mix well.

Serve the sauce cold. It can be stored in a covered container in the refrigerator for 3–4 days.

Makes 1¼ cups (10 fl oz/310 ml)

Tomato Sauce

This simple sauce is called for in two recipes in this book. It can also be spooned over fish before baking or after broiling. If you like, stir in chopped fresh herbs and sautéed garlic just before using. The sauce can be covered and refrigerated for up to 1 week. The recipe can also be easily halved.

5 cups (2 lb/1 kg) canned plum (Roma) tomatoes with their juices
1 cup (8 fl oz/250 ml) canned tomato purée
3 tablespoons unsalted butter or olive oil
salt and freshly ground pepper

In a food processor fitted with the metal blade, process the tomatoes and their juices until finely chopped but not liquefied.

Transfer to a nonreactive saucepan and stir in the tomato purée. Place over low heat and simmer, stirring often, until the sauce is slightly thickened, 20–30 minutes. Stir in the butter or oil and season to taste with salt and pepper.

Makes about 6 cups (48 fl oz/1.5 l)

Tomato Sauce

Tartar Sauce

Jalapeño Salsa

Nothing could be simpler. Serve on broiled or grilled fish and accompany with black beans and rice or grilled corn on the cob rubbed with chili powder and lime. The salsa can be dressed up with one of the following: 1 cup (6 oz/185 g) peeled, seeded and diced tomato; 1 cup (6 oz/185 g) peeled and diced papaya, mango, pineapple or avocado; or fresh orange juice or grated orange zest to taste.

¾ cup (4 oz/125 g) finely chopped onion
3 or 4 cloves garlic, finely minced
4–6 fresh jalapeño peppers, finely minced
¼ cup (2 fl oz/60 ml) fresh lime or lemon juice
2 tablespoons red or white wine vinegar or sherry
   vinegar
2 tablespoons olive oil
4 tablespoons chopped fresh cilantro (fresh coriander)
salt

Combine all the ingredients in a bowl, including salt to taste. Using a spoon or whisk, beat until thoroughly incorporated.

  Serve at room temperature, or cover and refrigerate for no more than 1 day.

Makes about 1 cup (8 fl oz/250 ml), enough for 4 servings

Salsa Verde

Here is a classic Mediterranean sauce that varies ever so slightly from country to country depending upon which herb is used, if the anchovy goes in, and whether lemon juice or vinegar is added. Chopped fresh mint, tarragon or basil can be used for part of the parsley. Spoon the sauce over grilled or poached fish. It is especially simpatico with meaty fish like tuna or swordfish, but works well on milder poached cod or sea bass, too.

3 tablespoons finely chopped yellow or white onion
2 cloves garlic, finely minced
½ cup (¾ oz/20 g) chopped fresh flat-leaf (Italian)
   parsley
2 tablespoons capers, rinsed and coarsely chopped
3 tablespoons red wine vinegar or fresh lemon juice
½ cup (4 fl oz/125 ml) extra-virgin olive oil
salt and freshly ground pepper
1 tablespoon finely minced anchovy fillet, optional

In a small bowl combine all the ingredients, including salt and pepper to taste and the anchovy, if desired. Using a spoon or large whisk, beat until thoroughly combined.

  Serve at room temperature, or cover and refrigerate for no more than 1 day.

Makes about 1 cup (8 fl oz/250 ml), enough for 4 servings

Jalapeño
Salsa

Salsa Verde

Fish Curry

3 tablespoons olive oil

2 yellow onions, chopped (about 2 cups/
    8 oz/250 g)

1 tablespoon grated fresh ginger

1 teaspoon finely minced garlic

1 teaspoon grated lime zest

1 teaspoon dried lemongrass or 1 stalk
    fresh lemongrass, chopped

2 tablespoons ground coriander

½ teaspoon cayenne pepper

1 teaspoon ground turmeric

1½ cups (12 fl oz/375 ml) coconut milk

1 tablespoon fresh lemon juice

1½ lb (750 g) firm white fish fillets such
    as cod, halibut, monkfish (anglerfish),
    snapper, flounder or sea bass, cut into
    2-inch (5-cm) cubes

salt

2 tablespoons chopped fresh mint

2 tablespoons chopped fresh basil

This is a cross between an East Indian and Southeast Asian curry. The base for the curry can be made a few hours ahead and the fish added and cooked just before serving. If you like ginger, increase the amount to 2 tablespoons. If you can't find lemongrass, add 1 teaspoon grated lemon zest and increase the lemon juice to 3 tablespoons. The curry can also be expanded to be a meal in a bowl by adding 2 cups (16 fl oz/500 ml) chicken or fish stock (recipe on page 11) with the coconut milk and about 1½ cups each cut-up green beans (8 oz/250 g), shredded cabbage (5 oz/155 g), diced bell peppers (capsicums) (6 oz/185 g), and diced zucchini (courgettes) or yellow crookneck squash (8 oz/250 g), before adding the fish. Serve with steamed rice and a favorite chutney.

*I*n a large saucepan or wide sauté pan over medium heat, warm the olive oil. Add the onions and sauté, stirring, until tender and translucent, about 10 minutes.

Add the ginger, garlic, lime zest, lemongrass, coriander, cayenne pepper and turmeric and sauté for 3–4 minutes longer.

Add the coconut milk and lemon juice, bring to a boil and immediately reduce the heat to a simmer. Simmer, uncovered, for 3 minutes, then add the fish cubes and cook until the fish is opaque throughout when tested with a knife, 5–8 minutes. Season to taste with salt.

Transfer to a serving dish. Garnish with the mint and basil and serve immediately.

Serves 4

Poached Whole Salmon

court bouillon (see note for fish stock, page 11)

1 whole salmon, about 5 lb (2.5 kg), cleaned

thinly sliced cucumber, dill sprigs or fennel feathers for garnish

If you do not have a fish poacher (see pages 6–7), wrap the salmon in cheesecloth (muslin), which will make it easier to retrieve, and rig a large pan with a rack and a cover. (If the salmon is too long to fit comfortably in the poacher or alternative pan, cut off the head and tail.) You can poach salmon fillets in a large sauté pan with a lid. They will take 8–10 minutes if they are 1 inch (2.5 cm) thick; adjust the cooking time according to their thickness. Serve poached salmon warm with hollandaise sauce (recipe on page 12) or an herbed vinaigrette, or chilled with aïoli (page 12) or tartar sauce (page 14).

Pour the court bouillon into a fish poacher with the rack in place (the bouillon must be deep enough to immerse the fish completely) and bring to a boil. Place the salmon in the poacher, lower the heat, cover and simmer until the salmon is opaque throughout when tested with a knife, 8–10 minutes per inch (2.5 cm) of thickness at its thickest point.

Lift out the rack and let the salmon cool until it can be touched. Then, carefully peel off the skin from the top side (it will come off easily) and pull out the fins from the flesh. Gently turn the salmon over, slipping it onto a large platter as you do. Peel off the skin from the second side. Serve at once, or let cool and serve at room temperature or chilled. Garnish with cucumber slices, dill sprigs or fennel feathers. To serve, cut halfway through the fish to the bone, into portions about 2 inches (5 cm) wide. Using a spatula, carefully lift the fish away from the bones.

Serves 5 or 6

Steamed Fish with Ginger and Green Onions

4 fish fillets, 5–6 oz (155–185 g) each
   (see note)

¼ cup (2 fl oz/60 ml) dry sherry

4 green (spring) onions, including tender
   green tops, finely minced

3 tablespoons grated fresh ginger

3 tablespoons soy sauce

2 teaspoons grated lemon or orange zest,
   optional

This fat-free method of cooking is ideal for flaky white fish fillets such as sea bass, snapper or rock cod or firm fish like salmon. The resultant flavors are clean and light. A whole fish can be steamed in the same way: Make 3 or 4 shallow diagonal cuts in the fleshiest part of both sides of the fish. Place on an aluminum foil-lined steamer rack and steam 15–20 minutes for a small fish, or 8–10 minutes per inch (2.5 cm) of thickness for a larger fish. Serve with rice and snow peas (mangetouts), gai lan *(Chinese broccoli),* bok choy *or asparagus.*

*P*lace the fish fillets on a double thickness of heavy-duty aluminum foil on a steamer rack, or place them on a heatproof plate and set the plate on the rack.

In a small bowl stir together the sherry, green onions, ginger, soy sauce and the zest, if using. Spread evenly atop the fish.

Bring water to a boil in a steamer pan. Place the rack in the steamer (make sure the water does not touch the rack). Cover and steam until the fish is opaque throughout when tested with a knife, 8–10 minutes for thin fillets and slightly longer for thicker ones.

Serves 4

Salmon Poached in Red Wine with Caramelized Shallots

16 shallots with stem ends intact, cut in half lengthwise

4 cloves garlic, unpeeled

1 tablespoon sugar

1 bay leaf

1 cinnamon stick, about 2 inches (5 cm) long

2 whole cloves

½ teaspoon freshly ground pepper

1½ bottles (4½ cups/36 fl oz/1.1 l) full-bodied red wine such as Côtes du Rhône or Zinfandel

4 salmon fillets, 5–6 oz (155–185 g) each

4 tablespoons (2 oz/60 g) unsalted butter

If you cannot find shallots, use yellow onions or leeks and cut into thick slices; you will need about 3½ cups (14 oz/440 g). Serve with steamed spinach and plain boiled potatoes or, better yet, mashed potatoes.

Combine the shallots, garlic cloves, sugar, bay leaf, cinnamon stick, cloves and pepper in a wide saucepan or deep sauté pan. Add 1½–2 cups (12–16 fl oz/375–500 ml) of the red wine, or as needed to cover the shallots. Simmer, uncovered, over low heat until the shallots are tender and the wine is reduced by half, about 30 minutes.

Remove from the heat and discard the garlic, bay leaf, cinnamon and cloves. Reserve the shallots and wine mixture.

In a large, deep sauté pan, pour in the remaining wine as needed to a depth of about 1 inch (2.5 cm) and bring to a simmer over low heat. Add the salmon fillets, cover and poach gently until opaque throughout when tested with a knife, 6–8 minutes.

Using a slotted utensil, transfer the salmon to a warmed platter and cover with plastic wrap to keep warm.

Bring the poaching liquid to a boil and reduce over high heat until quite syrupy, 8–15 minutes.

Add the reserved shallot mixture and then stir in the butter, 1 tablespoon at a time. Spoon the shallot mixture over the salmon and serve at once.

Serves 4

Italian Fish Stew

2–3 lb (1–1.5 kg) firm white fish fillets such as rockfish, sea bass, monkfish (anglerfish), cod, flounder or halibut

salt and freshly ground pepper

¼ cup (2 fl oz/60 ml) olive oil

3 yellow onions, chopped (2½–3 cups/ 10–12 oz/315–375 g)

2 green bell peppers (capsicums), seeded, deribbed and chopped (about 1 cup/5 oz/155 g)

3–6 cloves garlic, finely minced

½–2 teaspoons red pepper flakes, optional

2 teaspoons fennel seeds

2 teaspoons dried oregano

1 bay leaf

3–4 cups (18–24 oz/560–750 g) drained, canned plum (Roma) tomatoes, coarsely chopped, or 4 or 5 large, ripe tomatoes, peeled, seeded and coarsely chopped

2 cups (16 fl oz/500 ml) dry white or red wine

2 cups (16 fl oz/500 ml) fish stock (recipe on page 11) or bottled clam juice

4 tablespoons chopped fresh flat-leaf (Italian) parsley

4 tablespoons chopped fresh basil, optional

Called zuppa di pesce, *this is a typical Italian tomato-and-wine-based fish stew. The wine can be white or red, the herbs can be varied, and the amount of garlic and hot pepper is up to you. To take this to France, add a few strips of orange zest and ½ teaspoon saffron threads. To give it a Spanish accent, add ⅓ cup (1½ oz/45 g) finely chopped toasted almonds. The stew can be prepared several hours ahead of serving, up to the point where the fish is added; at mealtime, reheat the base and add the fish. Serve with polenta or lots of grilled or toasted bread. A green salad after would be nice.*

Cut the fish into uniform chunks 2–3 inches (5–7.5 cm) long. Place in a shallow nonreactive dish and sprinkle with salt and pepper. Cover and refrigerate while making the broth.

In a large, heavy saucepan over medium heat, warm the olive oil. Add the onions and bell peppers and cook, stirring, until tender, about 10 minutes.

Add the garlic, red pepper flakes (if using), fennel seeds, oregano and bay leaf and cook for 2 minutes. Add the tomatoes and simmer for 3 minutes longer. Add the wine and stock and simmer, uncovered, for another 10 minutes.

Season to taste with salt and pepper. Add the fish and simmer, uncovered, until opaque throughout when tested with a knife, 5–8 minutes. Add the parsley and the basil, if using. Serve at once.

Serves 4–6

Salmon with Mushrooms and Tarragon Cream

¼ cup (2 oz/60 g) unsalted butter

¾ lb (375 g) fresh mushrooms, thinly sliced

2 cups (16 fl oz/500 ml) dry white wine or dry vermouth, or as needed

4 salmon or sole fillets, 5–6 oz (155–185 g) each

1 cup (8 fl oz/250 ml) heavy (double) cream

2 tablespoons chopped fresh tarragon

salt and freshly ground pepper

Fast and easy and very French. The tarragon cream and mushrooms are a perfect foil for the moist fish fillets. Don't forget to wipe the mushrooms with a damp towel to remove grit; do not immerse them in water or they will lose their tasty juices too quickly.

*I*n a large sauté pan over medium-high heat, melt the butter. Add the mushrooms and sauté until just tender, 3–5 minutes. Transfer the mushrooms and their accumulated juices to a dish and set aside.

Pour the white wine or vermouth into the pan to a depth of about 1 inch (2.5 cm). Bring to a boil over high heat. Reduce the heat to medium-low and add the salmon or sole fillets. Cover and poach the fish until opaque throughout when tested with a knife, about 8 minutes for salmon and slightly less for sole, as sole fillets are thinner.

Using a slotted spatula, transfer the fillets to a warmed platter and cover with plastic wrap to keep warm.

Raise the heat to high and reduce the pan juices to a syrupy glaze, 5–8 minutes. Stir in the reserved mushrooms, the cream and tarragon and continue to cook for 1–2 minutes to reduce a bit. Season to taste with salt and pepper. Spoon the mushroom sauce over the fillets and serve immediately.

Serves 4

Caldo de Perro

2 tablespoons olive oil

2 yellow onions, chopped (about 2 cups/
    8 oz/250 g)

2 cloves garlic, finely minced

grated zest of 1 orange

4 cups (32 fl oz/1 l) fish stock *(recipe on
    page 11)*

1½ lb (750 g) firm white fish fillets such
    as cod, halibut, monkfish (anglerfish),
    snapper, flounder or sea bass, cut into
    2-inch (5-cm) chunks

8 small new potatoes, unpeeled, boiled
    until tender and halved (optional)

4 cups (8 oz/250 g) shredded Swiss
    chard or spinach (optional)

½ cup (4 fl oz/125 ml) fresh orange juice

¼ cup (2 fl oz/60 ml) fresh lime juice

salt and freshly ground pepper

*This is a simple and fragrant citrus-based fish soup from Spain.
Include the potatoes and greens to turn it into a complete meal.
To accentuate the flavor of the broth, accompany with 1 cup
(8 fl oz/250 ml) aïoli (recipe on page 12) to which you have added
3 tablespoons each fresh orange juice and grated orange zest.
Diners can spoon in the aïoli to taste. Offer grilled or toasted
bread at the table.*

*I*n a large sauté pan over medium heat, warm the olive oil.
Add the onions and sauté, stirring, until tender and
translucent, about 10 minutes. Add the garlic and orange
zest and sauté for 3 minutes longer.

Add the fish stock and bring to a boil. Reduce the heat and
simmer, uncovered, for 10 minutes. Add the fish and
simmer until opaque throughout when tested with a knife,
5–8 minutes.

Using a slotted spoon, transfer the fish to 4 large soup
bowls. Add the cooked potatoes and greens, if using, to the
pan and cook until the greens wilt and the potatoes are
warmed through. Remove the potatoes and greens and
divide equally among the soup bowls.

Stir the orange and lime juices into the soup base and
adjust the seasoning with salt and pepper. Ladle the soup
base over the fish, potatoes and greens. Serve at once.

Serves 4

Fish and Corn Chowder

2 tablespoons olive oil

6 oz (185 g) pancetta or bacon, cut into ½-inch (12-mm) pieces

2 yellow onions, chopped (about 2 cups/ 8 oz/250 g)

4 cups (32 fl oz/1 l) fish stock *(recipe on page 11)* or bottled clam juice

6–8 small red potatoes, unpeeled, cut into ½-inch (12-mm) chunks

1½ lb (750 g) cod or flounder fillets, cut into 1-inch (2.5-cm) cubes

2 cups (12 oz/375 g) corn kernels

1 cup (8 fl oz/250 ml) heavy (double) cream

salt and freshly ground pepper

2 tablespoons unsalted butter, optional

chopped fresh flat-leaf (Italian) parsley or thyme for garnish

This variation on the classic New England clam or scallop chowder uses firm white fish. It will taste best when made with fresh sweet corn, but no one will be upset if, in the dead of winter when you crave this hearty soup, you add thawed frozen corn. The smoky taste of bacon or the sweetness of pancetta is a nicer touch than the more traditional salt pork, as they accent the sweetness of the corn.

*I*n a large saucepan over medium-low heat, warm the olive oil. Add the pancetta or bacon and the onions and cook, stirring occasionally to prevent sticking, for 10 minutes.

Add the stock or clam juice and bring to a boil over high heat. Reduce the heat to medium and add the potatoes. Simmer, uncovered, until the potatoes are almost completely cooked through but still firm, 8–10 minutes. Add the fish and simmer for 4 minutes. Add the corn kernels and simmer about 3 minutes longer.

Stir in the cream and season to taste with salt and pepper. Swirl in the butter, if using. Top with chopped thyme or parsley and serve immediately.

Serves 4

Moroccan Tagine of Fish with Lemon and Olives

1½ lb (750 g) firm white fish fillets such as cod, snapper, halibut, flounder or sea bass, cut into 2-inch (5-cm) pieces

FOR THE MARINADE:
2 teaspoons paprika
½ teaspoon ground ginger
1 teaspoon ground cumin
¼ teaspoon cayenne pepper
2 tablespoons chopped fresh mint
2 tablespoons chopped fresh cilantro (fresh coriander) or flat-leaf (Italian) parsley
2 tablespoons fresh lemon juice
¼ cup (2 fl oz/60 ml) olive oil

FOR THE TAGINE BASE:
2 large lemons, thinly sliced
3 tablespoons olive oil
2 cups (8 oz/250 g) diced yellow onion
1 tablespoon paprika
1 teaspoon ground ginger
1 teaspoon ground turmeric
1 teaspoon ground cumin
¼ teaspoon cayenne pepper
2 cups (16 fl oz/500 ml) fish stock (recipe on page 11)
24 green olives, preferably pitted
salt and freshly ground pepper
chopped fresh flat-leaf (Italian) parsley and cilantro or mint for garnish

While this tagine (stew) usually is prepared with chicken or lamb, there is no reason why the pungent spices and tart lemon will not work with a rich fish. Serve with couscous and harissa, the fiery-hot Moroccan condiment. Look for both in specialty-food shops or in stores specializing in North African foods.

*P*lace the fish pieces in a nonreactive dish.

In a small bowl stir together all the ingredients for the marinade. Rub the marinade into the fish pieces. Cover and refrigerate for about 2 hours.

Meanwhile, to make the tagine base, place the lemon slices in water to cover, bring to a simmer and simmer, uncovered, for 5 minutes. Drain and place in a bowl. Add cold water to cover and let stand for 1 hour.

In a large sauté pan or saucepan over medium heat, warm the olive oil. Add the onion and sauté, stirring, until tender and translucent, about 10 minutes.

Add all the spices and cook, stirring, for about 5 minutes longer. Add the fish stock and bring to a boil. Reduce the heat to medium. Drain the lemon slices and add to the pan along with the fish. Simmer, uncovered, until the fish is opaque throughout when tested with a knife, 5–8 minutes.

Stir in the olives; taste and adjust the seasoning. Transfer to a serving dish and top with chopped parsley and cilantro or mint. Serve immediately.

Serves 4

Fillet of Sole with Lemon and Butter

½ cup (2½ oz/75 g) all-purpose (plain) flour

salt and freshly ground pepper

1½ lb (750 g) sole fillets

6 tablespoons (3 oz/90 g) clarified unsalted butter, plus 2 tablespoons regular unsalted butter

2 tablespoons fresh lemon juice

chopped fresh flat-leaf (Italian) parsley for garnish

Called à la meunière *in French, this lemon and butter treatment is the simplest, fastest and arguably most popular way to prepare fillet of sole. If you like, add 2 tablespoons capers, rinsed, with the lemon juice. For sole amandine, stir in 1 cup (4 oz/125 g) slivered blanched almonds with the 2 tablespoons butter and fry until the almonds are golden and the sauce is bubbly. Spoon over the fish and serve with lemon wedges. Serve fillet of sole with roast or steamed potatoes and spinach or broccoli. This recipe also works well for whole trout.*

Spread the flour on a plate and season with salt and pepper. Dip the fish fillets in the seasoned flour to coat completely. Shake off any excess.

Heat the 6 tablespoons (3 oz/90 g) clarified butter in a large sauté pan over medium-high heat. Working in batches, add the sole fillets and sauté quickly, turning once, until golden brown on both sides, about 2 minutes on each side. Using a slotted spatula, transfer the fish to warmed individual plates or a warmed platter.

Stir the lemon juice into the pan juices and then stir in the 2 tablespoons regular butter to enrich the sauce. Pour the sauce over the fish, top with chopped parsley and serve at once.

Serves 4 or 5

Sautéed Fish with Roasted Pepper and Sun-Dried Tomato Purée

2 large red bell peppers (capsicums)

4 tablespoons (2 fl oz/60 ml) olive oil

2 teaspoons finely minced garlic

¼ cup (1½ oz/45 g) well-drained,
   oil-packed sun-dried tomatoes, finely
   minced

2 teaspoons fresh lemon juice

1 teaspoon grated lemon zest

¼ teaspoon cayenne pepper, or to taste

about ½ cup (4 fl oz/125 ml) chicken
   or fish stock, or as needed *(recipe on
   page 11)*

salt and freshly ground pepper

4 firm white fish fillets, such as sea bass,
   monkfish (anglerfish) or rock cod, or
   flaky fish fillets such as sole, 5–6 oz
   (155–185 g) each

2–3 tablespoons unsalted butter,
   optional

4 tablespoons chopped fresh chives
   or mint

For extra richness use part unsalted butter for sautéing the fillets.

Hold the bell peppers over an open flame, or slip under a preheated broiler (griller). Turn until lightly blackened on all sides. Transfer to a covered plastic container for about 20 minutes. Peel away the blackened skin, cut the peppers in half, and seed and derib. Dice finely and set aside.

In a sauté pan over low heat, warm 2 tablespoons of the oil. Add the garlic and sauté for a few minutes, then stir in the sun-dried tomatoes. Add the diced peppers, lemon juice, zest and cayenne pepper. Cook, stirring, to blend the flavors, about 5 minutes. Purée in a food processor fitted with metal blade or in a blender. Add 2 tablespoons stock and process to spoonable consistency; add stock as needed. Season with salt and pepper. Set aside.

In a large sauté pan over medium heat, warm the remaining 2 tablespoons oil. Sprinkle the fish fillets with salt and pepper and add to the pan. Sauté, turning once, until golden on both sides and opaque throughout when tested with a knife, about 4 minutes on each side. Using a spatula transfer to warmed individual plates, cover with plastic wrap and keep warm.

Pour the remaining stock (⅓–½ cup/3–4 fl oz/80–125 ml) into the pan over high heat and deglaze by stirring to dislodge any browned bits. Reduce the heat to medium and add the purée; warm through. Swirl in the butter, if desired, or a little more stock to achieve a sauce consistency. Pour over the fish, sprinkle with the chives or mint and serve at once.

Serves 4

Deep-Fried Fish

1 cup (8 fl oz/250 ml) milk

1 egg, lightly beaten

1 cup (5 oz/155 g) all-purpose (plain) flour, or as needed

salt and freshly ground pepper

1 tablespoon curry powder or ½ teaspoon cayenne pepper, optional

1½ lb (750 g) firm white fish fillets (*see note*), cut into strips 2 inches (5 cm) long and 1 inch (2.5 cm) wide

1 cup (4 oz/125 g) fine cracker crumbs or fine dried bread crumbs, optional

peanut or corn oil for deep-frying

lemon wedges or tartar sauce (*recipe on page 14*) for serving

Lean, firm-fleshed fish is the best for deep-frying. Sole and cod— traditional choices for British fish and chips—are especially good. Small whole fish such as whitebait may also be used; they need only be coated with seasoned flour before frying. The ideal temperature for deep-frying is 375°F (190°C); the fish will cook and take on a golden color rather than brown too quickly and remain raw in the center. If using crackers for coating, finely crushed soda crackers work well. Serve the fried fish with French fries.

In a bowl combine the milk and egg and beat lightly to mix. Spread the flour on a plate and season with salt and pepper. Add the curry powder or cayenne pepper, if using.

Dip the fish in the egg-milk mixture, then in the seasoned flour. Place on a rack for 10 minutes to drain and to set the coating. Or coat the fish with flour, dip in the egg-milk mixture, and then coat with the cracker or bread crumbs. Place on a wire rack for 10 minutes to set the coating.

Preheat an oven to 275°F (135°C). In a wide saucepan, pour in oil to a depth of 3 inches (7.5 cm) and heat to 375°F (190°C) on a deep-frying thermometer, or until a small piece of bread turns golden within a few moments of being dropped into the oil. Add the fish, a few pieces at a time, and fry until golden brown, 3–4 minutes. Using a slotted spoon, transfer to paper towels to drain briefly, then place on a warmed ovenproof platter. Put into the oven to keep warm until all the fish is fried.

Serve the fish hot with lemon wedges or tartar sauce.

Serves 4–6

Stir-Fried Fish in Spicy Sichuan Sauce

4 tablespoons (2 fl oz/60 ml) dry sherry

2 tablespoons soy sauce

1 lb (500 g) firm white fish fillets such as cod, flounder or monkfish (anglerfish), cut into strips 2 inches (5 cm) long by 1 inch (2.5 cm) wide

¼ cup (2 fl oz/60 ml) ketchup or bottled chili sauce

1 teaspoon red pepper flakes

2 teaspoons sugar

½ teaspoon salt

2 tablespoons minced fresh ginger

1 tablespoon minced garlic

4–6 tablespoons (1 oz/30 g) finely minced green (spring) onion, including tender green tops

3 tablespoons peanut oil

Organize all of your ingredients in little bowls before you begin to cook. Accompany the stir-fry with steamed rice and broccoli, snow peas (mangetouts) or bok choy, or broiled or sautéed slender Asian eggplants (aubergines) and asparagus.

*I*n a shallow nonreactive dish, stir together 2 tablespoons of the sherry and 1 tablespoon of the soy sauce. Add the fish strips and toss to coat evenly. Marinate, uncovered, for about 30 minutes at room temperature.

In a small bowl stir together the ketchup or chili sauce and red pepper flakes; set aside. In another small bowl stir together the remaining 2 tablespoons sherry and 1 table-spoon soy sauce, the sugar and salt; set aside. In yet another bowl stir together the ginger, garlic and green onion; set aside.

In a large sauté pan or wok over high heat, warm the oil. Add the fish strips and ginger-garlic mixture and toss rapidly for about 2 minutes. Add the sherry mixture and continue to toss rapidly for 1 minute. Add the ketchup mixture and toss for 1 minute longer. Transfer to a warmed platter and serve immediately.

Serves 2 or 3

Sautéed Fish with Garlic, Rosemary and Chili Pepper

1½ lb (750 g) monkfish (anglerfish)
   fillets, cut on the diagonal into slices
   1 inch (2.5 cm) thick, or swordfish or
   tuna fillets, about 1 inch (2.5 cm) thick
salt and freshly ground pepper
¼ cup (2 fl oz/60 ml) olive oil
1 tablespoon red pepper flakes
2 tablespoons chopped fresh rosemary
1 tablespoon finely minced garlic
1 cup (8 fl oz/250 ml) dry white wine

This fish dish from Italy's Abruzzi region is fast and easy. Traditionally prepared with monkfish, it would be equally good with another firm, meaty fish such as tuna or swordfish. Serve with orecchiette or another favorite pasta, or with broccoli or sautéed greens such as Swiss chard.

Sprinkle the fish with salt and pepper. In a large sauté pan over medium-high heat, warm the olive oil. Working in batches, add the fish and sauté on both sides, turning once, until golden brown and almost cooked through, about 3 minutes on each side. (If using tuna fillets, they may be cooked less, to your taste.) Transfer the fish to a warmed platter.

Reduce the heat to medium and stir in the red pepper flakes, rosemary, garlic and wine. Simmer, uncovered, until the wine is reduced by half and becomes somewhat syrupy, about 5 minutes.

Return the fish to the pan for 1 or 2 minutes to coat it with the sauce, then serve at once.

Serves 4

Sautéed Fillet of Sole with Oranges

about 1 cup (5 oz/155 g) all-purpose (plain) flour

salt and freshly ground pepper

1½ lb (750 g) sole fillets

3 tablespoons clarified unsalted butter, plus 1–2 tablespoons regular unsalted butter

¼ cup (1½ oz/45 g) finely chopped yellow onion

⅓ cup (3 fl oz/80 ml) dry white wine

½ cup (4 fl oz/125 ml) fresh orange juice

2 teaspoons grated orange zest

2 oranges, peeled, white membrane removed and sectioned

chopped fresh flat-leaf (Italian) parsley or mint for garnish

Simple and tasty, this dish is Spanish in inspiration. Serve with spinach or with asparagus topped with toasted almonds. Accompany with plain white rice or saffron rice.

Preheat an oven to 275°F (135°C).

Spread the flour on a plate and season with salt and pepper. Coat the fillets lightly with the flour and shake off any excess.

In a large sauté pan over medium-high heat, melt the 3 tablespoons clarified butter. Add the fish and sauté, turning once, until browned on both sides and opaque throughout when tested with a knife, 2–3 minutes on each side. Using a slotted spatula, transfer the fish to a warmed ovenproof platter or 4 ovenproof plates and cover with aluminum foil. Place in the oven to keep warm.

Reduce the heat to medium, add the onion and sauté, stirring, until tender and translucent, 5–8 minutes. Add the wine and orange juice and zest, raise the heat to high and cook, uncovered, until reduced by half, 5–8 minutes. Season to taste with salt and pepper and stir in the 1–2 tablespoons butter and the orange sections. Heat until warmed through.

Pour the sauce over the fish. Sprinkle with parsley or mint and serve immediately.

Serves 4 or 5

Salmon Risotto

5 cups (40 fl oz/1.25 l) chicken stock or
  half chicken stock and half fish stock
  (recipe on page 11)
¼ cup (2 fl oz/60 ml) olive oil or
  unsalted butter
1 lb (500 g) salmon fillets, cut into strips
  2 inches (5 cm) long by 1 inch
  (2.5 cm) wide
salt and freshly ground pepper
¼ cup (2 oz/60 g) unsalted butter
1 yellow onion, diced (about 1¼ cups/
  5 oz/155 g)
1½ cups (10½ oz/330 g) Arborio rice
1 cup (5 oz/155 g) shelled peas
6 cups (6 oz/185 g) spinach leaves,
  carefully washed and cut into thin
  strips, or a combination of spinach and
  watercress leaves
2 teaspoons grated lemon zest
2 tablespoons finely minced fresh chives

For additional crunch, add 1 cup (5 oz/155 g) diced fennel with the last addition of stock and ½ cup (2½ oz/75 g) toasted pine nuts with the chives.

*P*our the stock into a saucepan and bring to a boil. Reduce the heat and keep at a simmer.

In a wide sauté pan over medium-high heat, warm the oil or butter. Sprinkle the fish strips with salt and pepper and add to the pan. Sauté quickly, turning to brown lightly, about 3 minutes. The fish will not be fully cooked. Set aside.

In a wide, heavy saucepan over medium heat, melt the ¼ cup (2 oz/60 g) butter. Add the onion and sauté, stirring occasionally, until translucent, about 10 minutes.

Reduce the heat, add the rice and stir to coat with the butter. Cook, stirring, until the rice is opaque, 3–5 minutes.

Add ½ cup (4 fl oz/125 ml) of the hot stock, stir and simmer, uncovered, until the stock is absorbed. Continue adding stock, ½ cup (4 fl oz/125 ml) at a time and allowing it to be fully absorbed before adding more, until the rice is almost cooked. Stir occasionally to prevent sticking.

Meanwhile, fill a saucepan three-fourths full with water and bring to a boil. Add the peas and boil until lightly cooked, 1–4 minutes depending upon their age and size. Drain well.

During the last addition of stock to the rice, add the spinach and lemon zest and cook, stirring, until the spinach wilts. Stir in the salmon, peas and chives and warm through. Season with salt and pepper and serve at once.

Serves 4

Pasta with Fresh Tuna

6 tablespoons (3 fl oz/90 ml) olive oil

1 lb (500 g) tuna fillet, 1 inch (2.5 cm) thick

salt and freshly ground pepper

1 lb (500 g) dried pasta such as penne, orecchiette, spaghetti or linguine

1 cup (4 oz/125 g) diced red (Spanish) onion

2 tablespoons finely minced garlic

2 teaspoons dried oregano

1 tablespoon red pepper flakes

2 cups (16 fl oz/500 ml) tomato sauce (*recipe on page 14*)

12 Kalamata olives, pitted and coarsely chopped

6 tablespoons (½ oz/15 g) chopped fresh flat-leaf (Italian) parsley, plus extra chopped parsley for garnish

If you have only canned tuna on hand, add 2 cans (7 oz/220 g each) tuna at the same point you would add the fresh tuna. (If using water-packed tuna, drain well; if using olive oil–packed tuna, do not drain.) Garnish the pasta with lots of fresh parsley. But no cheese, please.

*I*n a large sauté pan over medium-high heat, warm 2–3 tablespoons of the oil. Add the tuna and sear quickly, turning to brown on both sides, 2–3 minutes per side. Season to taste with salt and pepper and set aside. Alternatively, preheat a broiler (griller), or prepare a fire in a charcoal grill. Brush the tuna lightly with 2–3 tablespoons oil and sprinkle with salt and pepper. Place the tuna on a broiler pan or a grill rack. Broil or grill, turning once, until cooked to desired doneness, 2–3 minutes on each side for medium-rare. (The tuna will cook slightly more in the sauce.)

Let the tuna cool slightly and then cut into strips 1 inch (2.5 cm) long and ½ inch (12 mm) wide.

Bring a large pot of salted water to a boil. Drop in the pasta and stir well to separate. Cook until al dente. The timing will depend upon the type of pasta; follow package directions.

Meanwhile, warm the remaining 3–4 tablespoons oil in a large sauté pan over medium heat. Add the onion and sauté until translucent but not soft, about 5 minutes. Add the garlic, oregano and red pepper flakes and warm through. Add the tomato sauce and bring to a simmer. Add the tuna and warm through. Remove from the heat and add the olives and the 6 tablespoons (½ oz/15 g) parsley. Season with salt and pepper.

Drain the pasta and place in a warmed pasta bowl. Add the tuna sauce and toss well. Garnish with parsley. Serve at once.

Serves 4

Sautéed Tuna in a Crunchy Cumin Crust

FOR THE MARINADE:

½ cup (4 fl oz/125 ml) olive oil

¼ cup (2 fl oz/60 ml) fresh lemon juice

1 tablespoon grated fresh ginger

1 teaspoon minced garlic

1 teaspoon finely minced fresh jalapeño pepper

4 tuna fillets, each 5–6 oz (155–185 g) and 1 inch (2.5 cm) thick

FOR THE RAITA:

1 cup (8 oz/250 g) nonfat yogurt, drained in a sieve for 3 hours

½ cup (3 oz/90 g) peeled, seeded and diced tomatoes

½ cup (2½ oz/75 g) peeled, seeded and diced cucumber

3 tablespoons finely chopped green (spring) onion

salt and freshly ground pepper

FOR THE CRUST:

¼ cup (2 oz/60 g) cumin seeds

¾ cup (3 oz/90 g) fine dried bread crumbs

3 tablespoons olive oil

An Indian-inspired fish sauté. The raita topping is a nice foil for the crispy fish. Note that you must drain the yogurt for 3 hours before you mix it with the other ingredients; otherwise the topping will be too thin. Chopped fresh mint or cilantro (fresh coriander) can be substituted for the green onion in the raita. Serve with saffron rice and grilled eggplant (aubergine).

To make the marinade, in a shallow nonreactive dish, stir together all the ingredients. Add the tuna and turn to coat evenly. Cover and marinate for 1 hour at room temperature.

To make the *raita,* in a bowl combine all the ingredients and stir until well mixed. Set aside.

To make the crust, place the cumin seeds in a small, dry frying pan over medium-low heat. Toast the seeds, shaking the pan, until fragrant, about 5 minutes. Transfer to a mortar and crush finely with a pestle.

Combine the bread crumbs and crushed cumin seeds on a plate. Remove the tuna from the marinade and coat on both sides with the cumin mixture.

In a large, heavy sauté pan over high heat, warm the olive oil. Add the fish and sauté quickly, turning once, until golden brown and cooked to desired degree of doneness, about 2 minutes on each side for medium-rare.

Transfer to warmed individual plates and top with the *raita.* Serve at once.

Serves 4

Fish Paprikash

⅔ cup (3½ oz/110 g) all-purpose (plain) flour

1 teaspoon salt, plus salt to taste

½ teaspoon freshly ground pepper, plus pepper to taste

1 teaspoon plus 2 tablespoons sweet paprika

1½ lb (750 g) firm white fish fillets (see note), cut into strips about 2 inches (5 cm) long and 1 inch (2.5 cm) wide

4 tablespoons (2 fl oz/60 ml) olive oil

2 large yellow onions, cut into slices ¼ inch (6 mm) thick

2 green bell peppers (capsicums), seeded, deribbed and cut into long strips ¼ inch (6 mm) wide

¼–½ teaspoon cayenne pepper

2 cups (12 oz/375 g) drained, seeded and diced canned plum (Roma) tomatoes

¼ cup (2 fl oz/60 ml) sour cream, at room temperature

This Hungarian-inspired dish is traditionally made with carp, but a mild white fish such as flounder, sturgeon or cod can also be used. Unsalted butter or a combination of olive oil and butter can be substituted for the olive oil. Serve with rice, noodles or with the small dumplings called spaetzle.

On a plate mix together the flour, 1 teaspoon salt, ½ teaspoon ground pepper and 1 teaspoon paprika. Coat the fish strips evenly with the flour mixture.

In a large sauté pan over high heat, warm 2–3 tablespoons of the olive oil. Working in batches, add the fish strips and brown quickly, turning once; the fish should be somewhat underdone. Using a slotted spatula, transfer to a platter.

Wipe the pan with paper towels and place over medium heat. Add 1–2 tablespoons of the olive oil, heat and add the onions. Sauté for 5 minutes, stirring occasionally, then add the bell peppers and cook, stirring, until softened, another 5–8 minutes.

Stir in the 2 tablespoons paprika and the cayenne pepper and cook, stirring, for 2 minutes. Add the tomatoes and bring to a simmer. Season to taste with salt and pepper. Return the fish to the pan and simmer, uncovered, until warmed through, about 3 minutes.

Remove from the heat and swirl in the sour cream. Serve at once.

Serves 4

Tuna Steak with Cracked Peppercorns

¼ cup (2 oz/60 g) unsalted butter, softened

2 tablespoons fresh lemon juice

2 teaspoons grated lemon zest

salt

3 tablespoons olive oil

2 tablespoons cracked pepper

4 tuna steaks, each about 6–8 oz (185–250 g) and 1½ inches (4 cm) thick

Tuna is a meaty fish, quite like steak in texture. This recipe is a variation on a classic beef dish called steak au poivre. *It is simplicity itself and may become your favorite way to serve this prime fish. The redder the tuna, the better and moister the result will be. You may also sauté the tuna steaks in olive oil in a hot frying pan instead of broiling them; cook them 3–4 minutes on each side. Serve with French fries and green beans.*

Preheat a broiler (griller).

In a small bowl combine the butter, lemon juice and zest and salt to taste. Whisk until thoroughly combined. Set aside.

Pour the olive oil onto a plate. Place the cracked pepper on another plate. Dip the tuna in the oil and then press some cracked pepper onto both sides of each steak. Sprinkle with salt.

Place the steaks on a broiler pan and broil (grill), turning once, until cooked to desired degree of doneness, 2–3 minutes on each side for medium-rare.

Serve immediately with the lemon butter.

Serves 4

Trout with Prosciutto and Sage

4 trout or Coho salmon trout, cleaned
   and boned with heads intact, about
   10 oz (315 g) each
salt and freshly ground pepper
12 fresh sage leaves
4 large, thin slices prosciutto
olive oil
5 tablespoons (2½ oz/80 g) unsalted
   butter
grated zest of 1 lemon
2 tablespoons fresh lemon juice
1 teaspoon freshly ground pepper

A northern Italian recipe that couldn't be simpler, and it looks pretty, too. Ask your fishmonger to prepare the trout for cooking. Serve with fried potatoes and spinach, asparagus or green beans.

Preheat a broiler (griller), or prepare a fire in a charcoal grill.

Using a sharp knife, cut a few shallow diagonal slashes in the fleshiest part of each side of each fish. Sprinkle with a little salt and pepper. Place 3 sage leaves in the cavity of each fish and then wrap each fish in a slice of prosciutto.

Brush each trout on both sides with a little olive oil. Place on a broiler pan or grill rack. Broil or grill, turning once, until the prosciutto is browned and the fish is opaque throughout when tested with a knife, 4–5 minutes on each side.

Meanwhile, in a small pan melt the butter and season with the lemon zest and juice and the pepper.

Transfer the fish to warmed individual plates and spoon a little of the butter sauce over each fish. Serve immediately.

Serves 4

Fish with Walnut, Mint and Basil Pesto

⅔ cup (¾ oz/20 g) firmly packed basil
  leaves

½ cup (½ oz/15 g) firmly packed mint
  leaves

3 tablespoons walnuts, toasted and
  coarsely chopped

½ cup (4 fl oz/125 ml) mild-flavored
  olive oil, plus extra oil for brushing

½ teaspoon salt, plus salt to taste

¼ teaspoon freshly ground pepper, plus
  pepper to taste

2 tablespoons fresh lemon juice, or to
  taste

2 teaspoons grated lemon zest, optional

4 fish fillets (see note), 5–6 oz (155–
  185 g) each

This herb purée with the crunch of nuts is ideal for a firm white fish such as sea bass or halibut or a meaty fish such as tuna or swordfish. The pesto can be made 4–6 hours ahead (the color will darken over time), refrigerated and brought to room temperature at serving time. You must never cook the pesto, for heat turns it an unsightly brown. Roast potatoes and zucchini (courgettes) or asparagus are complementary accompaniments.

*I*n a food processor fitted with the metal blade or in a blender, place the basil, mint and walnuts. Pulse briefly to combine. Add ¼ cup (2 fl oz/60 ml) of the olive oil and pulse briefly again just to combine. Add the remaining oil and process to a coarse purée. Add the ½ teaspoon salt, the ¼ teaspoon pepper and the lemon juice and zest and pulse to combine. You should have about 1½ cups (12 fl oz/375 ml) pesto.

Preheat a broiler (griller), or prepare a fire in a charcoal grill.

Brush the fish fillets on both sides with olive oil. Sprinkle with salt and pepper. Place the fish on a broiler pan or on a grill rack. Broil or grill, turning once, until opaque throughout when tested with a knife, 3–4 minutes on each side. (If using tuna fillets, they may be cooked less, to your taste.)

Transfer to warmed individual plates and spoon the pesto over the fish. Serve immediately.

Serves 4

Fish in Grape Leaves

½ cup (4 fl oz/125 ml) extra-virgin
  olive oil

4 tablespoons (2 fl oz/60 ml) fresh lemon
  juice

2 tablespoons chopped fresh dill, parsley
  or oregano, plus extra for serving

4 fish fillets such as salmon, swordfish,
  sea bass or rockfish, 5–6 oz (155–
  185 g) each

8 large grape leaves, rinsed, patted dry
  and tough stems removed

freshly ground pepper

1 cup (6 oz/185 g) peeled, seeded and
  diced tomatoes, optional

2 teaspoons grated lemon zest or
  orange zest

In countries where grapes are grown, the vine leaves are used to wrap food cooked on the grill, imparting a certain smoky flavor and protecting delicate fish from breaking or sticking to the grill. Look for grape leaves packed in brine in jars; they can be found in stores selling Greek and Middle Eastern foods and in well-stocked food markets. If you want, you can also bake leaf-wrapped fish in an oven preheated to 450°F (230°C) for about 8 minutes. Serve with rice pilaf or bulgur pilaf and grilled eggplant (aubergine) and bell peppers (capsicums).

*I*n a shallow nonreactive container, mix together ¼ cup (2 fl oz/60 ml) of the olive oil, 2 tablespoons of the lemon juice and the 2 tablespoons chopped herb. Add the fish, turn to coat evenly and marinate for about 30 minutes at room temperature.

Preheat a broiler (griller) or prepare a fire in a charcoal grill. Wrap each fish fillet in 2 grape leaves. You may secure the leaves with toothpicks, but it is probably unnecessary. Sprinkle the wrapped fish with pepper and brush with some of the remaining olive oil. Place the fish on a broiler pan or on a grill rack. Broil or grill, turning once, 3–4 minutes on each side.

Transfer to a serving platter. Spoon the remaining oil and the remaining 2 tablespoons lemon juice over the fish packets. Top with the tomatoes, if desired, and citrus zest and more herbs. Serve at once.

Serves 4

Broiled Fish in Indian Ginger Masala

4 meaty fish fillets such as tuna, shark or
swordfish, or firm white fish fillets
such as halibut, sea bass or flounder,
5–6 oz (155–185 g) each

1 piece fresh ginger, about 2 inches
(5 cm) long, peeled and sliced

6 cloves garlic, chopped

2 or 3 fresh jalapeño peppers, seeded
and sliced

1 large yellow onion, diced (about 1¼
cups/5 oz/155 g)

1 teaspoon ground turmeric

¼ cup (2 fl oz/60 ml) fresh lemon juice,
white wine vinegar or rice vinegar

¼ cup (2 fl oz/60 ml) olive oil, plus extra
oil for brushing

salt and freshly ground pepper

lime or lemon wedges for serving

This zesty Indian spice rub will perk up the blandest white fish or stand up to a meaty fish like tuna. Do not marinate for more than an hour, or the acidity of the ginger will break down the texture of the fish. Serve with rice and lentils or cauliflower braised in a curried onion and tomato base. Or accompany with saffron rice and sautéed spinach.

Place the fish fillets in a shallow nonreactive dish.

In a blender or in a food processor fitted with the metal blade, combine the ginger, garlic, jalapeños and onion. Purée until smooth. Add the turmeric and lemon juice or vinegar and blend well. Transfer to a bowl and stir in the ¼ cup (2 fl oz/60 ml) olive oil; season to taste with salt.

Pour this mixture evenly over the fish fillets. Cover and marinate for 1 hour at room temperature.

Preheat a broiler (griller) or prepare a fire in a charcoal grill. Remove the fish fillets from the marinade and brush on both sides with olive oil. Sprinkle with salt and pepper. Place the fish on a broiler pan or on a grill rack. Broil or grill, turning once, until opaque throughout when tested with a knife, about 4 minutes on each side. (If using tuna, it may be cooked less, to your taste.) Serve immediately with lime or lemon wedges.

Serves 4

Broiled Mackerel or Tuna with Mustard

4 mackerel fillets or tuna steaks, 5–6 oz
  (155–185 g) each
olive oil
salt and freshly ground pepper
½ cup (4 oz/125 g) Dijon mustard
grated orange or lemon zest, optional
2 tablespoons fresh lemon juice

If you are using mackerel fillets, you can top the mustard mixture with ½ cup (2½ oz/75 g) grated yellow onion before returning the fillets to the broiler. Then broil, basting with a little olive oil, until the onion is golden and the mustard topping is crusty, about 4 minutes. Serve with lemon or orange wedges. Green beans, carrots or a leafy green like spinach or Swiss chard are a nice foil for the rich fish. Partner with simple potatoes or rice.

Preheat a broiler (griller). Oil a broiler pan.

Place the fish fillets or steaks on the prepared broiler pan. Brush with olive oil and sprinkle with salt and pepper. Broil (grill) for 4 minutes on the first side.

Meanwhile, in a small bowl stir together the mustard, zest, if using, and lemon juice. Turn the fish fillets over and spread the mustard mixture evenly on the tops. Sprinkle with salt and pepper.

Broil until the fish is crusty and medium-done, about 4 minutes longer.

Serves 4

Middle Eastern Grilled Swordfish

1 yellow onion, coarsely chopped

2 cloves garlic, chopped

1 tablespoon ground coriander

2 teaspoons sweet paprika

pinch of cayenne pepper

¼ cup (2 fl oz/60 ml) fresh lemon juice

2 teaspoons coarsely chopped fresh
  thyme or oregano

½ cup (4 fl oz/125 ml) olive oil, plus
  extra oil for brushing

4 swordfish steaks, 5–6 oz (155–185 g)
  each

salt and freshly ground pepper

A fast and easy marinade for broiled fish. Any firm white fish such as sea bass or cod can be substituted for the swordfish. Serve with rice pilaf and broiled eggplant (aubergine), zucchini (courgettes) or sautéed spinach.

In a food processor fitted with the metal blade or in a blender, combine the onion, garlic, coriander, paprika, cayenne pepper and lemon juice. Purée until smooth and transfer to a bowl. Stir in the thyme or oregano and the ½ cup (4 fl oz/125 ml) olive oil.

Place the swordfish steaks in a shallow nonreactive container and pour the mixture over the fish to coat evenly. Cover and marinate for 2–4 hours in the refrigerator.

Preheat a broiler (griller), or prepare a fire in a charcoal grill.

Remove the fish steaks from the marinade. Brush the steaks on both sides with olive oil and sprinkle with salt and pepper. Place the fish on a broiler pan or grill rack. Broil or grill, turning once, until opaque throughout when tested with a knife, about 4 minutes on each side. Serve at once.

Serves 4

North African Fish Kabob

3 cloves garlic, finely minced

1 tablespoon ground cumin

1 teaspoon freshly ground pepper, plus
    pepper to taste

3 tablespoons fresh lemon juice

⅓ cup (3 fl oz/80 ml) olive oil, plus extra
    oil for brushing

4 tablespoons chopped fresh mint

2 tablespoons chopped fresh marjoram

pinch of cayenne pepper, optional

1½ lb (750 g) fish fillets such as
    swordfish, snapper, mackerel or tuna,
    cut into ¾–1-inch (2–2.5-cm) cubes

salt

You can use this picante marinade for a whole fish as well: Cut a few shallow diagonal slashes in the fleshiest part of the fish on both sides and rub well with the marinade. Place in a shallow glass or ceramic dish, cover and marinate for 1 hour at room temperature or 3–5 hours in the refrigerator. Serve the cooked fish with couscous or with roast or fried potatoes sprinkled with a little ground cumin and freshly ground pepper. Carrots, green beans or fennel would be nice accompaniments.

*In a shallow nonreactive dish, mix together the garlic, cumin, pepper, lemon juice, the ⅓ cup (3 fl oz/80 ml) olive oil, mint, marjoram and the cayenne pepper, if using. Add the fish cubes and toss to coat well. Cover and marinate for 1 hour at room temperature or in the refrigerator for 2–3 hours.

    Preheat a broiler (griller), or prepare a fire in a charcoal grill.

    Thread the fish onto bamboo or metal skewers (if using bamboo, soak the skewers in water for 30 minutes to prevent burning). Brush the fish with a little olive oil. Sprinkle with salt and pepper. Place on a broiler pan or grill rack. Broil or grill, turning once, until opaque throughout when tested with a knife, about 4 minutes on each side. (If using tuna, it may be cooked less, to your taste.) Serve at once.

Serves 4

Broiled Fish in a Greek Marinade

5 tablespoons (3 fl oz/80 ml) olive oil
1½ tablespoons finely minced garlic
1 tablespoon dried oregano
2 teaspoons chopped fresh thyme
grated zest of 1 lemon
2 tablespoons fresh lemon juice
¼ cup (2 fl oz/60 ml) ouzo or other
　anise-flavored liqueur
salt and freshly ground pepper
4 firm fish fillets such as swordfish or
　sea bass, 5–6 oz (155–185 g) each
lemon wedges for serving

The flavors of the Aegean permeate this dish. If you cannot find ouzo, the Greek anise-flavored liqueur, French Pernod will add a similar perfume. This marinade would work well on a whole fish such as a 2½–3 lb (1.25–1.5 kg) snapper or rock cod. Just cut a few shallow diagonal slashes in the fleshiest part on both sides so that the fish can absorb the marinade, then cook for 5–6 minutes on each side. Serve with panfried potatoes topped with crumbled feta cheese and chopped Kalamata olives.

In a small sauté pan over low heat, warm 4 tablespoons (2 fl oz/60 ml) of the olive oil. Add the garlic and oregano and simmer for about 2 minutes. Remove from the heat and transfer to a bowl. Stir in the thyme, lemon zest and juice, ouzo or other liqueur, and salt and pepper to taste. Let cool completely.

　Place the fish fillets in a shallow nonreactive container and pour the mixture over the fish. Turn the fish a few times to coat evenly. Cover and marinate for 2–3 hours in the refrigerator.

　Preheat a broiler (griller), or prepare a fire in a charcoal grill. Remove the fish from the marinade and brush with the remaining 1 tablespoon olive oil. Place on a broiler pan or on a grill rack. Broil or grill, turning once, until opaque throughout when tested with a knife, about 4 minutes on each side. Transfer to a warmed platter and garnish with lemon wedges. Serve at once.

Serves 4

Baked Fish alla Veracruzana

4 snapper fillets, 5–6 oz (155–185 g)
  each
¼ cup (2 fl oz/60 ml) olive oil
2 yellow onions, sliced
4 cloves garlic, minced
2 teaspoons dried oregano
2 teaspoons chili powder
pinch of ground cinnamon
4 fresh jalapeño peppers, or more to
  taste, finely chopped
2 cups (12 oz/375 g) drained and
  chopped canned plum (Roma)
  tomatoes or 6 fresh plum tomatoes,
  peeled and coarsely chopped
grated zest of 1 lemon or lime
2 tablespoons fresh lemon juice
salt and freshly ground pepper
3 tablespoons chopped fresh flat-leaf
  (Italian) parsley
¼ cup (1¼ oz/40 g) pimiento-stuffed
  olives

While this is the classic Mexican snapper preparation, there is no reason why cod, sea bass or halibut could not be served in the same way. Accompany the fish with steamed potatoes and olives.

Preheat an oven to 400°F (200°C). Lightly oil a baking dish in which the fish fillets will fit in a single layer. Bring the fish to room temperature.

In a large sauté pan over medium heat, warm the ¼ cup (2 fl oz/60 ml) olive oil. Add the onions and sauté, stirring, until tender and translucent, about 10 minutes. Add the garlic, oregano, chili powder, cinnamon, jalapeños, tomatoes and citrus zest and juice. Simmer, uncovered, for 5 minutes longer. Taste and adjust the seasoning.

Sprinkle the fish fillets with salt and pepper. Place in the prepared baking dish and pour the sauce evenly over the top. Bake until the fish is opaque when tested with a knife, about 15 minutes.

Transfer to a warmed platter. Sprinkle with the parsley and garnish with the olives. Serve immediately.

Serves 4

Middle Eastern Baked Fish with Nut and Sesame Crust

2 cloves garlic, chopped

½ cup (2½ oz/75 g) chopped almonds or hazelnuts (filberts), toasted

6 tablespoons (3½ oz/105 g) tahini

¼ cup (2 fl oz/60 ml) fresh lemon juice

½ teaspoon salt, plus salt to taste

4 firm white fish fillets such as snapper, cod, sea bass or flounder, 5–6 oz (155–185 g) each

1–2 tablespoons olive oil

freshly ground pepper

2 tablespoons sesame seeds

2 tablespoons chopped fresh flat-leaf (Italian) parsley

While this sesame sauce is usually spread on cooked fish and served at room temperature, it is even better spread on the fish before baking, because it keeps it moist. The sauce may be made several hours ahead of time but will thicken considerably; thin with water to restore its spreadability. Tahini, a thick sesame seed paste, can be found in Middle Eastern food shops and in well-stocked food markets. Serve this dish with roast potatoes or cracked-wheat pilaf and spinach or zucchini (courgettes). Garnish with lemon wedges and olives, if you like.

*P*ut the garlic and nuts in a blender or in a food processor fitted with the metal blade and process to mince the nuts finely. Add the tahini and lemon juice and purée. Add just enough cold water to form a spreadable paste and process until smooth. Season with the ½ teaspoon salt.

Preheat an oven to 450°F (230°C). Bring the fish to room temperature.

Use the olive oil to oil a baking dish large enough to hold the fish fillets in a single layer. Place the fish in the dish and sprinkle with salt and pepper. Spread the tahini mixture over the fish fillets. Bake for 10–15 minutes.

Meanwhile, place the sesame seeds in a small, dry frying pan and toast over medium heat, shaking the pan occasionally, until fragrant, 3–4 minutes. Sprinkle the fish with the parsley and toasted sesame seeds and serve at once.

Serves 4

Baked Fish with Fennel, Orange Zest and Pernod

1 teaspoon fennel seeds

3 tablespoons olive oil

1 large yellow onion, thinly sliced (about 6 oz/185 g)

2 large fennel bulbs, cored and thinly sliced lengthwise (about 4 cups/1 lb/ 500 g)

1 tablespoon grated orange zest

2 cups (12 oz/375 g) peeled, seeded and diced tomatoes, optional

salt and freshly ground pepper

4 cod, flounder or sea bass fillets, about 5–6 oz (155–185 g) each

1 cup (8 fl oz/250 ml) dry white wine

¼ cup (2 fl oz/60 ml) Pernod

fennel feathers or chopped fresh mint for garnish

Here, sliced fennel and orange zest make a fragrant bed for firm white fish fillets. Including tomatoes results in a more complex and substantial blend. The addition of fennel seeds and of Pernod, a popular anise-based spirit bottled in France, complements the sweet anise flavor of the fresh fennel. Serve with roast potatoes.

*P*lace the fennel seeds in a small, dry frying pan over medium-low heat and toast, shaking occasionally, until fragrant, 4–5 minutes. Transfer to a mortar and pulverize with a pestle. Alternatively, pulverize in a spice grinder.

Preheat an oven to 450°F (230°C).

In a large sauté pan over medium heat, warm the olive oil. Add the onion and sauté, stirring, until tender and translucent, about 10 minutes. Add the sliced fennel and sauté for 3–4 minutes. Add the ground fennel seeds, orange zest and the tomatoes, if using, and cook for 2 minutes longer. Season to taste with salt and pepper.

Distribute the fennel mixture among 4 individual baking dishes or place in 1 large baking dish. Place the fish fillets atop the fennel. Sprinkle with salt and pepper. In a cup or bowl combine the wine and Pernod and pour over the fish.

Bake until the fish is opaque when tested with a knife, about 8 minutes. Sprinkle with fennel feathers or mint and serve at once.

Serves 4

Fish in Parchment

¼ cup (2 fl oz/60 ml) olive oil, plus extra
    oil for brushing
2 large yellow onions, sliced
grated zest of 1 large orange
grated zest of 1 lemon
4 tablespoons chopped fresh mint
¼ cup (2 fl oz/60 ml) fresh orange juice
2 tablespoons fresh lemon juice
salt and freshly ground pepper
4 flaky white fish fillets such as sole or
    cod, 5–6 oz (155–185 g) each

This makes for an impressive but easy dinner. The fish packets can be assembled hours ahead of time and refrigerated. Let each diner open his or her own packet so that the first perfumes of the dish fill the dining room rather than the kitchen. Serve with steamed rice or roast potatoes and broccoli or green beans.

Preheat an oven to 475°–500°F (245°–260°C).

Fold 2 sheets of parchment paper in half lengthwise. Starting at the fold, cut out 2 heart-shaped pieces from each sheet, making each heart about 2 inches (5 cm) wider than the fish fillets. Set aside.

In a sauté pan over medium heat, warm the ¼ cup (2 fl oz/ 60 ml) olive oil. Add the onions and sauté until tender, about 10 minutes. Add the orange and lemon zests and mint; sauté for 3 minutes. Add the orange and lemon juices and sauté for 2 minutes longer. Season with salt and pepper.

Open the paper hearts flat on a work surface. Brush the paper with a little oil. Place a fish fillet atop one side of each heart, close to the fold. Sprinkle the fish with salt and pepper and top with the onion mixture. Fold the paper to enclose the fish and roll the edges to seal. Place the packets on a baking sheet. Bake until the parchment is puffed and browned, about 12 minutes.

Open one packet and test the fish with a knife point; it should be opaque. (That packet will be yours, of course.) Transfer to individual plates and serve at once.

Serves 4

Roast Fish with Saffron Rice Stuffing

3 tablespoons unsalted butter, plus
  melted butter or olive oil for basting
½ cup (2 oz/60 g) diced yellow onion
¼ cup (1 oz/30 g) minced green (spring)
  onion, including tender green tops
1 cup (7 oz/220 g) long-grain white rice
2 cups (16 fl oz/500 ml) hot water
½ teaspoon saffron threads, steeped in
  2 tablespoons dry white wine
1 snapper, salmon or rock cod, 5–6 lb
  (2.5–3 kg), cleaned
¼ cup (1 oz/30 g) golden raisins,
  plumped in hot water for 20–30
  minutes and well drained (optional)
½ teaspoon ground cinnamon
grated zest of 1 large orange
2 teaspoons chopped fresh thyme or dill
salt and freshly ground pepper

The optional raisins will add a pleasant sweetness to the stuffing. Serve with spinach and carrots seasoned with cinnamon and dill. Baked butternut squash also makes a nice accompaniment.

*I*n a sauté pan over medium heat, melt the 3 tablespoons butter. Add the yellow onion and sauté until tender, about 10 minutes. Add the green onion and sauté for 2 minutes. Add the rice, hot water and saffron and wine, stir well and bring to a boil. Reduce the heat to low, cover and cook until the liquid is absorbed, 15–20 minutes.

Meanwhile, preheat an oven to 400°F (200°C). Oil a baking dish large enough to accommodate the fish. Bring the fish to room temperature.

Remove the rice from the heat. Fold in the raisins, if using, and the cinnamon, orange zest and thyme or dill. Season to taste with salt and pepper. Let cool completely.

Spoon the rice into the fish cavity and skewer closed. Place the fish in the prepared dish. Bake, basting occasionally with melted butter or oil, until the fish tests done, 8–10 minutes per inch (2.5 cm) of thickness or about 40 minutes' total cooking time. To test, open a slit near the bone with a knife to see if the fish is cooked through and flaky. Or insert a metal skewer into the thickest part of the fish to the bone; if it feels hot on the tongue, the fish is done.

Transfer the fish to a warmed platter and serve at once.

Serves 4

Turbans of Sole

3 tablespoons unsalted butter

¼ cup (1 oz/30 g) minced green (spring) onion, including tender green tops

½ lb (250 g) fresh mushrooms, coarsely chopped

1 tablespoon all-purpose (plain) flour

salt and freshly ground pepper

freshly grated nutmeg

8 sole fillets, 3–4 oz (90–125 g) each

about 2 cups (16 fl oz/500 ml) dry white wine or dry vermouth

1 cup (8 fl oz/250 ml) heavy (double) cream

½ cup (2 oz/60 g) grated Swiss cheese

¼ cup (1 oz/30 g) freshly grated Parmesan cheese

The mushroom filling, cream and cheese make this a rich but festive dish. It can be assembled 3 hours ahead of time and refrigerated. If you can find only large sole fillets, split them lengthwise. Serve with steamed new potatoes or rice and peas.

$\prec$

*P*reheat an oven to 400°F (200°C).

In a sauté pan over medium heat, melt the butter. Add the green onion and sauté for 2 minutes. Add the mushrooms, raise the heat and cook until they give off some liquid, a couple of minutes. Stir in the flour to thicken a bit and season with salt, pepper and nutmeg. Set aside to cool. (This mixture can be made a day ahead, covered and refrigerated.)

Spread each sole fillet with some of the mushroom mixture and roll up. Skewer in place with a toothpick.

Pour the wine or vermouth into a large sauté pan with a lid that fits well. The liquid should be about ½ inch (12 mm) deep. Bring to a simmer and add the sole rolls, standing them upright. Cover and cook until the sole is opaque and just firm but not fully cooked, 5–7 minutes; the centers should be only half-cooked. Using a slotted spatula carefully transfer the rolls to a baking dish. Sprinkle with salt and pepper. Spread any extra mushroom mixture around the rolls.

Place the sauté pan holding the wine over high heat. Boil until reduced to ¾ cup (6 fl oz/180 ml). Swirl in the cream and reduce a bit more. You'll want about 1½ cups (12 fl oz/ 375 ml). Pour over the sole and top with the cheeses. Bake until browned and bubbly, 20–30 minutes. Serve very hot.

Serves 4

Roast Fish with Mediterranean Herbed Tomato Sauce

2–3 tablespoons olive oil

1 yellow onion, finely chopped (about 1 cup/5 oz/155 g)

2 cloves garlic, finely minced

1½ lb (750 g) tomatoes, peeled, seeded and chopped

salt and freshly ground pepper

pinch of sugar, if needed

6 tablespoons (½ oz/15 g) chopped fresh flat-leaf (Italian) parsley

4 tablespoons chopped fresh basil

2 tablespoons chopped fresh thyme

4 flaky white fish fillets such as cod, snapper, flounder or sea bass, 5–6 oz (155–185 g) each

A simple tomato sauce cloaks this basic baked fish. You can vary the taste of the dish by changing the herbs. For example, omit the thyme and use only parsley and basil, or omit the basil and add 1 tablespoon dried oregano or 2 tablespoons chopped fresh oregano or marjoram. Black or green olives, pitted and coarsely chopped, can be added to the sauce at the last minute and warmed gently. Serve with white beans and zucchini (courgettes), eggplant (aubergine) or sautéed greens such as Swiss chard. You might want to perk up the vegetables with a squeeze of lemon.

Preheat an oven to 450°F (230°C). Oil a baking dish in which the fish fillets will fit in a single layer.

In a saucepan or high-sided sauté pan over medium heat, warm the 2–3 tablespoons olive oil. Add the onion and sauté, stirring, until tender and translucent, about 10 minutes. Add the garlic and sauté for 1 or 2 minutes. Stir in the tomatoes and cook over low heat until the sauce thickens, 15–20 minutes.

Season to taste with salt and pepper. Taste the sauce; if the tomatoes are too sour, add the sugar. Stir in half of the parsley, basil and thyme and simmer for 2 minutes.

Place the fish in the prepared dish. Spoon the tomato sauce evenly over the top. Bake until the fish is opaque when tested with a knife, 8–10 minutes.

Remove from the oven and sprinkle with the remaining herbs. Serve at once.

Serves 4

Roast Fish with Sweet and Sour Onions

¼ cup (2 fl oz/60 ml) olive oil

5 cups (18 oz/560 g) sliced yellow
onions (about 4 large onions)

¼ teaspoon ground ginger

¼ teaspoon freshly grated nutmeg

¼ cup (1½ oz/45 g) currants, plumped
in hot water for 15–20 minutes
(optional)

¼ cup (2 fl oz/60 ml) red wine vinegar

2 tablespoons honey

1 tablespoon grated orange zest

1 teaspoon salt, plus salt to taste

½ teaspoon freshly ground pepper, plus
pepper to taste

4 firm white fish fillets such as sole,
snapper, cod or sea bass, 5–6 oz
(155–185 g) each

*This seasoned onion mixture is ideal to cover fish fillets for baking,
or use it to top fish cooked in parchment (recipe on page 79).
Check the fish for doneness after 5 minutes by inserting a knife
into the fillet. The fish will continue to cook if left in the baking
dish once it is out of the oven, so transfer immediately to
individual plates. Salmon fillets can be used for this dish. Sole
fillets will also work, but because they are thinner than most
fillets, they cook more quickly. Serve with potatoes or rice and
spinach, broccoli, green beans or asparagus.*

In a large sauté pan over medium heat, warm the olive oil.
Add the onions and cook, stirring occasionally, until tender
and translucent, about 10 minutes. Reduce the heat to low
and continue to cook the onions, uncovered, until they are
quite soft and sweet, 10–15 minutes longer.

Stir in the ginger and nutmeg and cook, stirring, for
1 minute. If using the currants, drain well and add to the pan
with the vinegar, honey and orange zest. Cook for 3 minutes
longer. Add the 1 teaspoon salt and ½ teaspoon pepper.

Meanwhile, preheat an oven to 450°F (230°C). Oil a
baking dish in which the fish fillets will fit in a single layer.

Place the fillets in the prepared dish and sprinkle lightly
with salt and pepper. Top with the seasoned onions. Bake
until the fish is opaque when tested with a knife, 7–9
minutes. Using a spatula transfer the fillets to warmed
individual plates. Serve at once.

Serves 4

Roast Fish with Almond and Bread Crumb Stuffing

2 tablespoons unsalted butter

½ cup (2 oz/60 g) diced yellow onion

½ cup (2½ oz/75 g) diced celery

2 cups (4 oz/125 g) fresh bread crumbs

4 tablespoons chopped fresh flat-leaf (Italian) parsley

1 tablespoon chopped fresh marjoram

2 teaspoons grated lemon zest

½ cup (2½ oz/75 g) toasted chopped almonds

salt and freshly ground pepper

1 sea bass or snapper, 4–5 lb (2–2.5 kg), cleaned

½ cup (4 fl oz/125 ml) melted unsalted butter or olive oil

What a treat to roast a whole fish! The stuffing is enriched with nuts for a pleasing crunch. Hazelnuts (filberts) can replace the almonds, and fresh corn bread crumbs can be used in place of regular fresh crumbs. You can substitute fresh fennel for the celery, in which case use tarragon or dill rather than marjoram. You may want to add sautéed mushrooms to the stuffing as well. Serve with roast or boiled potatoes and a leafy green vegetable.

Preheat an oven to 425°F (220°C). Oil a baking dish large enough to accommodate the fish.

In a sauté pan over medium heat, melt the butter. Add the onion and sauté for 5 minutes. Add the celery and sauté, stirring, for 3 minutes longer. Remove from the heat. Add the bread crumbs, parsley, marjoram, lemon zest and toasted almonds. Season to taste with salt and pepper. Stuff into the fish cavity and skewer closed. Place the fish in the prepared baking dish.

Bake the fish, basting occasionally with the melted butter or oil, until it tests done, 8–10 minutes per inch (2.5 cm) of thickness or about 40 minutes' total cooking time. To test, open a slit near the bone with a knife to see if the fish is cooked through and flaky. Or insert a metal skewer into the thickest part of the fish to the bone; if it feels hot on the tongue, the fish is done.

Carefully transfer to a warmed platter and serve immediately.

Serves 4

Roast Cod or Halibut with Belgian Endive, Walnuts and Cream

4 cod or halibut fillets, 5–6 oz
  (155–185 g) each, cut into strips
  2 inches (5 cm) long and 1 inch
  (2.5 cm) wide
salt
3 tablespoons olive oil
4 heads Belgian endive (chicory/witloof),
  cut crosswise thinly (about 8 cups
  loosely packed)
3 tablespoons balsamic vinegar
5 tablespoons (3 fl oz/80 ml) toasted
  walnut oil
freshly ground pepper
½ cup (4 fl oz/125 ml) heavy (double)
  cream
½ cup (2 oz/60 g) coarsely chopped
  walnuts, toasted

The bitterness of the endive contrasts nicely with the sweet cream and toasty nuts to enliven a mild white fish. As a variation, substitute leeks for the endive: Wash them carefully and slice, white parts only, to measure 8 cups (1½ lb/750 g). Sauté in the olive oil until tender, 10–15 minutes, then continue as directed.

Preheat an oven to 450°F (230°C). Place the fish in a shallow nonreactive dish and sprinkle with salt. Cover and refrigerate.

In a sauté pan over medium heat, warm the olive oil. Add the endive and cook, stirring, until wilted, 3–4 minutes. Stir in 1 tablespoon of the vinegar and 2 tablespoons of the walnut oil and cook, stirring, for 2 minutes longer. Season to taste with salt and pepper. Remove from the heat.

In a bowl whisk together the cream, the remaining 3 tablespoons walnut oil and the remaining 2 tablespoons balsamic vinegar. Season to taste with salt and pepper.

Distribute the endive mixture among 4 individual baking dishes or place in 1 large one. Top evenly with the fish strips. Season to taste with salt and pepper. Drizzle the seasoned cream evenly over the fish. Bake until the fish is opaque when tested with a knife, about 5 minutes.

Remove from the oven and top with the toasted walnuts. Serve immediately.

Serves 4

Baked Fish with Potatoes, Onions and Tomatoes

8–12 small red new potatoes
4 tablespoons olive oil
salt and freshly ground pepper
2 cups (8 oz/250 g) diced yellow onion
2 cloves garlic, finely minced
1 teaspoon dried oregano
2 cups (12 oz/375 g) peeled, seeded and
   diced fresh or drained canned plum
   (Roma) tomatoes
½ cup (4 fl oz/125 ml) dry white wine or
   fish stock *(recipe on page 11)*
pinch of ground cinnamon
4 firm white fish fillets such as cod, sea
   bass, flounder or halibut, 5–6 oz
   (155–185 g) each

FOR THE GRATIN TOPPING:
¾ cup (3 oz/90 g) toasted fine dried
   bread crumbs
½ cup (2 oz/60 g) freshly grated
   Parmesan cheese

3 tablespoons chopped fresh flat-leaf
   (Italian) parsley

Here is an ideal one-dish supper. The topping can be omitted; simply strew with more parsley when serving.

Arrange the potatoes on a steamer rack over boiling water. Cover and steam until half-cooked, about 10 minutes. Alternatively, boil the potatoes in water to cover until half-cooked, about 8 minutes; drain.

When the potatoes are cool enough to handle, slice cross-wise into rounds ¼ inch (6 mm) thick and place in a bowl.

Oil 4 individual or 1 large baking dish. Add 2 tablespoons of the olive oil to the potatoes, toss to coat and sprinkle with salt and pepper. Place the potatoes in the dish(es). Preheat an oven to 400°F (200°C).

In a sauté pan over medium heat, warm the remaining 2 tablespoons oil. Add the onion and sauté until tender, about 10 minutes. Add the garlic and oregano and cook for 2–3 minutes. Add the tomatoes, wine or stock and cinnamon; simmer briskly, uncovered, until slightly reduced, a few minutes. Season with salt and pepper.

Spoon half of the tomato mixture over the potatoes and top with the fish fillets. Sprinkle with salt and pepper. Top with the rest of the tomato mixture. In a small bowl, mix the bread crumbs and Parmesan and sprinkle on top.

Bake until the fish is opaque when tested with a knife and the potatoes are tender, 10–12 minutes. Sprinkle with the parsley and serve hot.

Serves 4

Tandoori Fish

1 small yellow onion, coarsely chopped

1 clove garlic, chopped

2 tablespoons thinly sliced fresh ginger

2 tablespoons fresh lemon or lime juice

2 teaspoons ground coriander

½ teaspoon cayenne pepper, or a bit less to taste

1 teaspoon ground cumin

¼ teaspoon ground cardamom

1 tablespoon paprika

½ teaspoon salt

1 cup (8 oz/250 g) nonfat plain yogurt

4 mild white fish fillets such as flounder, cod, sea bass, snapper or halibut, 5–6 oz (155–185 g) each

2 tablespoons chopped fresh cilantro (fresh coriander) or green (spring) onion, including tender green tops

Named for an Indian clay oven that cooks food at extremely high temperatures, this fish preparation can be grilled or broiled, although you may have problems with the fillets sticking to the grill. If you do decide to grill or broil the fish fillets, brush them well with oil, then cook for about 3 minutes on each side. Serve with saffron rice, broccoli and wedges of lemon or lime.

*I*n a food processor fitted with the metal blade or in a blender, combine the onion, garlic, ginger and citrus juice. Purée until smooth. Add all the spices and the yogurt and blend to combine.

Place the fish fillets in a nonreactive dish and pour the marinade evenly over the top. Cover and marinate for about 4 hours in the refrigerator.

Preheat an oven to 450°F (230°C). Bring the fish to room temperature.

Remove the fish from the marinade and place in a baking dish in which the fillets fit in a single layer. Bake until the fish is opaque when tested with a knife, 8–10 minutes.

Garnish with cilantro or green onion. Serve immediately.

Serves 4

Gravlax with Mustard-Dill Sauce

1 whole salmon fillet with skin intact, about 2 lb (1 kg)
3 tablespoons sugar
3 tablespoons kosher salt
½ teaspoon freshly ground pepper
½ teaspoon ground allspice, optional
24 dill sprigs
3–4 tablespoons aquavit, gin or vodka

FOR THE MUSTARD-DILL SAUCE:
¼ cup (2 oz/60 g) Dijon mustard
1 teaspoon dry mustard
2 tablespoons sugar
2 tablespoons distilled white vinegar
½ cup (4 fl oz/125 ml) peanut oil
2–3 tablespoons chopped fresh dill

Gravlax is salmon that has been cured with salt, sugar and aquavit. Because it must be served thinly sliced, start with a good-sized piece of salmon to make cutting easier. Aquavit, the Scandinavian caraway-flavored spirit, is the traditional curing liquor, but you can also use gin or vodka. Offer the gravlax as a first course with dark rye or pumpernickel bread. It will keep refrigerated for about 1 week.

Place the salmon skin-side down in a shallow nonreactive container. In a small bowl stir together the sugar, salt, pepper and the allspice, if using, and rub over the top surface of the salmon. Place the dill sprigs on top and sprinkle with the liquor. Cover with plastic wrap and place a heavy weight on top; a good choice is 3–4 lb (1.5–2 kg) canned goods placed inside another container. Refrigerate for 3–4 days, basting daily with the juices that accumulate.

When ready to serve, make the mustard-dill sauce: In a small food processor fitted with the metal blade or in a blender, combine the Dijon mustard, dry mustard, sugar and vinegar. Pulse to combine. With the motor running, slowly add the peanut oil and continue to process until the sauce thickens. Transfer to a bowl and fold in the dill.

To serve, remove and discard the dill sprigs. Slice the salmon thinly across the grain. Serve the sauce on the side.

Serves 8–12

Mediterranean Tuna Salad

FOR THE GARLIC VINAIGRETTE:

2 teaspoons dried oregano or 2 tablespoons minced fresh oregano

½ cup (4 fl oz/125 ml) mild-flavored olive oil

½ cup (4 fl oz/125 ml) extra-virgin olive oil

⅓ cup (3 fl oz/80 ml) red wine vinegar

3 tablespoons fresh lemon juice

2 cloves garlic, finely minced

4 tablespoons chopped fresh basil or mint (optional)

2 tablespoons capers, rinsed and coarsely chopped (optional)

2 tablespoons finely minced anchovy fillet in olive oil (optional)

1 lb (500 g) tuna fillet

olive oil for brushing

12 small new potatoes, unpeeled, boiled until tender, drained and cut in half or into thick rounds

4 ripe tomatoes, cut into quarters

1 lb (500 g) green beans, trimmed, boiled just until tender-crisp and plunged into cold water

2 hard-cooked eggs, cut into quarters

½ cup (2 oz/60 g) Niçoise or Kalamata olives

2 green bell peppers (capsicums), seeded, deribbed and sliced lengthwise

lettuce (optional)

When you order tuna salad in a Mediterranean village, you will likely get canned tuna. And that can be very good indeed if it is solid-pack albacore in good olive oil. You can even use 2 cans (7 oz/220 g each) tuna for making this salad. But since we can often find fresh tuna, why not take the time to cook a nice thick fillet? To achieve the correct balance of flavors, use a combination of mild-flavored pure olive oil and a fruitier extra-virgin olive oil. Take this salad in any direction you like by varying the optional additions to the vinaigrette.

Preheat a broiler (griller), or prepare a fire in a charcoal grill.

To make the vinaigrette, if using dried oregano place in a small, dry frying pan and toast over medium-low heat, shaking the pan occasionally, until fragrant, 2–3 minutes. Combine with all the remaining vinaigrette ingredients in a small bowl, including the basil or mint, capers and anchovy, if using. Whisk thoroughly; set aside.

Brush the tuna fillets on both sides with olive oil. Place on the broiler pan or grill rack. Broil or grill, turning once, to desired doneness, 2–3 minutes on each side for medium-rare. Alternatively, warm a little oil in a frying pan over medium heat. Add the tuna fillet and sauté, turning once, to desired doneness, 4–5 minutes on each side for medium-rare.

Let the tuna cool completely, then cut into 1–2-inch (2.5–5-cm) chunks. Arrange the tuna, potatoes, tomatoes, drained beans, eggs, olives and bell peppers on 4 individual plates, lined with lettuce if desired. Drizzle with the vinaigrette and serve.

Serves 4

Ceviche

1 lb (500 g) firm white fish fillets such as sea bass or snapper, cut into bite-sized pieces

½ cup (4 fl oz/125 ml) fresh lemon juice

½ cup (4 fl oz/125 ml) fresh lime juice

2–3 teaspoons finely minced fresh jalapeño pepper

1 teaspoon finely minced garlic

½ teaspoon salt

2 small red (Spanish) onions, sliced paper-thin

4 tablespoons chopped fresh cilantro (fresh coriander)

¼ cup (2 fl oz/60 ml) mild-flavored olive oil

1 or 2 tomatoes, peeled, seeded and diced (optional)

Ceviche is South America's answer to what to serve at the start of a meal. If sweet, vine-ripened tomatoes are in season, they make a colorful, flavorful addition. Mound atop lettuce leaves, or accompany with guacamole and crisp tortilla chips.

*I*n a shallow nonreactive dish, place the fish and pour in the lemon and lime juices. Toss gently. Cover and refrigerate for 2 hours.

Add all the remaining ingredients, including the tomatoes, if using. Toss gently to mix well. Cover and refrigerate until the fish "cooks" in the liquid and turns white, 1–2 hours longer. Serve chilled.

Serves 4

Smoked Trout, Avocado and Orange Salad

FOR THE GINGER VINAIGRETTE:

⅓ cup (1½ oz/45 g) peeled and sliced
  fresh ginger

¼ cup (2 fl oz/60 ml) fresh lemon juice

2 tablespoons white wine vinegar, or to
  taste

1 teaspoon sugar

⅔ cup (5 fl oz/160 ml) peanut oil

salt and freshly ground pepper

2 smoked trout, about 7 oz (220 g) each

1 red (Spanish) onion, sliced paper-thin

2 ripe but firm avocados

6 cups (6 oz/185 g) loosely packed
  spinach or watercress leaves or
  assorted greens, carefully washed

2 large navel oranges, peeled, white
  membrane removed and sectioned

A delightful way to start a meal, or serve as a centerpiece for a light summer lunch. Increase the amount of trout if you want a more filling salad. The vinaigrette can be made up to 6 hours in advance of serving.

To make the vinaigrette, place the ginger in a blender or in a food processor fitted with the metal blade and chop finely. Add the lemon juice and vinegar and process to form a fine purée. Transfer to a bowl and whisk in the sugar, peanut oil and salt and pepper to taste. You will have about 1¼ cups (10 fl oz/310 ml) vinaigrette.

To assemble the salad, skin and bone the trout. Separate the fillets, then tear them into bite-sized pieces. Set aside.

In a bowl combine the onion and ¼ cup (2 fl oz/60 ml) of the vinaigrette. Set aside for 15 minutes.

Cut the avocados in half. Remove the pits and peel the halves. Cut the avocado halves into long slices ¼ inch (6 mm) thick. Place in a bowl and drizzle with ¼ cup (2 fl oz/60 ml) of the vinaigrette.

In another bowl toss together the spinach or watercress and the onion slices and their vinaigrette with ½ cup (4 fl oz/125 ml) of the remaining vinaigrette. Distribute the greens among 4 salad plates. Place the orange segments and trout in the now-empty bowl with the remaining vinaigrette and toss well. Arrange the avocado slices, trout pieces and orange segments atop the greens and serve.

Serves 4

Glossary

The following glossary defines terms specifically as they relate to fish cookery, including major and unusual ingredients and basic techniques.

AQUAVIT
A clear, dry Scandinavian spirit distilled either from potatoes or grains and usually flavored with caraway, or sometimes with citrus and spices.

BASIL
Sweet, spicy herb popular in Italian and French cooking, particularly as a seasoning for tomatoes and tomato sauces.

BAY LEAVES
Dried whole leaves of the bay laurel tree. Pungent and spicy, they flavor simmered dishes, marinades and pickling mixtures. The French variety, sometimes available in specialty-food shops, has a milder, sweeter flavor than California bay leaves. Discard bay leaves before serving.

BELGIAN ENDIVE
Leaf vegetable with refreshing, slightly bitter spear-shaped leaves, white to pale yellow-green—or sometimes red—in color, tightly packed in cylindrical heads 4–6 inches (10–15 cm) long. Also known as chicory or witloof.

BELL PEPPER
Fresh, sweet-fleshed, bell-shaped member of the pepper family. Also known as capsicum. Most common in the unripe green form, although ripened red or yellow varieties are also available. Creamy pale-yellow, orange and purple-black types may also be found.

BOK CHOY
Chinese variety of cabbage with elongated crisp white stalks and dark green leaves, with a refreshing, slightly peppery flavor.

BREAD CRUMBS
To make bread crumbs, choose a good-quality, rustic-style loaf made of unbleached wheat flour, with a firm, coarse-textured crumb; usually sold in bakeries as country-style, rustic or peasant bread. For fresh bread crumbs, cut away the crusts from the bread and break the bread into coarse chunks. Put them in a food processor fitted with the metal blade or in a blender and process to desired consistency. For dried crumbs, spread the bread crumbs in a baking pan and leave in an oven set at its lowest temperature until they feel very dry, 30–60 minutes; do not let brown. Dried bread crumbs, usually fine-textured, are also sold prepackaged in food markets.

CAPERS
Small, pickled buds of a bush common to the Mediterranean, used whole as a savory flavoring or garnish.

CAYENNE
Very hot ground spice derived from dried cayenne chili peppers.

BUTTER
For the recipes in this book, unsalted butter is preferred. Lacking salt, it allows the cook greater leeway in seasoning recipes to taste.

Butter is often clarified—that is, its milk solids and water are removed—when it is to be used for cooking at higher temperatures or as a sauce.

To clarify butter, melt it in a small, heavy saucepan over very low heat; watch carefully to avoid burning. Remove from the heat and let sit briefly.

Then, using a spoon, skim off and discard the foam from the surface.

Finally, carefully pour off the clear yellow oil, leaving the milky solids and water behind in the pan.

CHILI POWDER
Commercial blend of spices featuring ground dried chili peppers along with such other seasonings as **cumin, oregano,** cloves, **coriander,** pepper and salt. Best purchased in small quantities, because flavor diminishes rapidly after opening.

CHILI SAUCE
Commercial bottled blend of hot and mild chili peppers, **vinegar,** sugar and other flavorings, used as a seasoning ingredient or as a condiment.

CILANTRO
Green, leafy herb resembling flat-leaf (Italian) **parsley,** with a sharp, aromatic, somewhat astringent flavor. Popular in Latin American and Asian cuisines. Also called fresh coriander and commonly referred to as Chinese parsley.

CLAM JUICE
The strained liquid of shucked clams, sold in small bottles in the fresh or canned seafood departments of food stores. Because of its refreshing briny flavor, the juice is often used as a cooking liquid for seafood dishes.

COCONUT MILK
Although commonly thought to be the thin, relatively clear liquid found inside a whole coconut, coconut milk is actually an extract made from shredded fresh coconut. Unsweetened coconut milk is available in cans in some food markets. Or make your own by steeping 1½ cups (4½ oz/ 140 g) unsweetened grated coconut in an equal amount of hot water, puréeing the mixture in a blender and then straining it through a sieve lined with cheesecloth (muslin), squeezing well to extract all the liquid.

CORIANDER
Small, spicy-sweet seeds of the coriander plant, which is also called **cilantro** or Chinese parsley. Used whole or ground as a seasoning, particularly in Middle Eastern and Indian cuisines.

CORNICHONS
French-style sour pickled cucumbers no more than about 2 inches (5 cm) in length. Available in specialty-food shops.

COURT BOUILLON
French for "short broth," describing a quickly prepared cooking liquid of aromatic vegetables and herbs simmered in water for about 30 minutes and used for poaching or otherwise moistening seafood recipes.

CREAM, HEAVY
Whipping cream with a butterfat content of at least 36 percent. For the best flavor and cooking properties, purchase 100 percent natural fresh cream with a short shelf life printed on the carton, avoiding long-lasting varieties that have been processed by ultra-pasteurization methods. In Britain, use double cream.

CUMIN
Middle Eastern spice with a strong, dusky, aromatic flavor, popular in cuisines of its region of origin along with those of Latin America, India and parts of Europe. Sold either ground or as whole, small, crescent-shaped seeds.

DILL
Herb with fine, feathery leaves and sweet, aromatic flavor well suited to pickling brines, vegetables, seafood, chicken, veal and pork. Sold fresh or dried.

FENNEL
Crisp, refreshing, mildly anise-flavored bulb vegetable, sometimes called by its Italian name, *finocchio*. Another related variety of the bulb is valued for its stems and fine fronds or "feathers," which are used as a fresh or dried herb; and for its small, crescent-shaped seeds, dried and used as a spice.

GINGER
The rhizome of the tropical ginger plant, which yields a sweet, strong-flavored spice. Whole ginger rhizomes, commonly but mistakenly called roots, may be purchased fresh in a food store or vegetable market. Ground dried ginger is easily found in jars or tins in the spice section of food stores.

GRAPE LEAVES
In Greek and other Middle Eastern cuisines, grapevine leaves are commonly used as edible wrappers. Most commonly found bottled in brine in ethnic delicatessens and the specialty-food section of well-stocked food markets; rinse gently and remove tough stems before use. If fresh leaves are available, briefly blanch or steam to soften them before use.

JALAPEÑO CHILI
Extremely hot fresh chili pepper with a distinctive sharp flavor. A small, tapering chili that measures about 1½ inches (4 cm) long and is usually dark green, although ripe red ones are occasionally available.

Hotness will vary depending on the chili's growing location and conditions and upon its precise strain. Because most of the heat resides in the pepper seeds and white pithy membranes, or ribs, taste a tiny piece of the chili's flesh before adding it to a recipe; if it is hot enough for your liking, remove the seeds and ribs (after removing the stem and slitting the pepper open), or include them if you prefer more fiery results.

Whenever cutting or chopping chilies, use kitchen gloves to protect hands from volatile oils if you have any cuts or abrasions; wash hands liberally with warm, soapy water after handling chilies, and avoid touching your eyes.

LEMONGRASS
Thick, stalklike grass with a sharp, lemony flavor, popular in Southeast Asian cooking and available fresh or dried in some Asian food stores.

If fresh lemongrass is unavailable, substitute 1 tablespoon dried lemongrass for each 8-inch (20-cm) stalk of fresh; or substitute long, thin strips of lemon peel.

MIRIN
Sweetened Japanese rice wine used as a flavoring ingredient. Medium-dry sherry may be substituted.

MUSTARDS
Mustard is available in three forms: whole seeds, powdered (referred to as dry mustard) and prepared, which is made from powdered or coarsely ground mustard seed mixed with liquid such as vinegar or wine. Spicy Dijon mustard is made in Dijon, France, from powdered dark brown mustard seeds (unless otherwise marked *blanc*) and white wine or wine vinegar. Pale in color, fairly hot and sharp tasting, true Dijon mustard and non-French blends labeled "Dijon-style" are widely available in most food markets and specialty-food stores.

NUTS, TOASTING
Toasting brings out the full flavor and aroma of nuts. To toast any kind of nut, preheat an oven to 325°F (165°C). Spread the nuts in a single layer on a baking sheet and toast in the oven until they just begin to change color, 5–10 minutes, depending upon their size. Remove from the oven and let cool to room temperature.

OILS
Oils not only provide a medium in which fish may be browned without sticking, but can also subtly enhance the flavor of recipes in which they are used. Extra-virgin olive oil, extracted from olives on the first pressing without use of heat or chemicals, is prized for its fruity taste and golden to pale green hue. "Pure" olive oil has a higher acidity and less defined flavor than extra-virgin oil. Many brands, varying in color and strength of flavor, are now widely available; choose one that suits your taste. For subtler, milder flavor, choose a paler green variety.

Pale gold peanut oil has a subtle hint of the peanut's richness. Golden corn oil has an almost undiscernible flavor and may be heated to a high temperature for all-purpose frying. Walnut oil has the rich flavor and color of the nut from which it is pressed, and is used as a seasoning and in salad dressings. Store all oils in airtight containers away from heat and light.

OLIVES
Throughout Mediterranean Europe, ripe black olives are cured in combinations of salt, seasonings, brines, vinegars and oils to produce pungently flavored results. Good-quality cured olives, such as French Niçoise or Greek Kalamata or Italian Gaeta varieties, are available in ethnic delicatessens, specialty-food shops and well-stocked supermarkets. Green olives are sometimes preferred for their sharper flavor; pitted, they are occasionally stuffed with strips of pickled red pimientos for a hint of color and sweetness.

To pit an olive, use a special olive pitter, which grips the olive and pushes out the pit in one squeeze. Or carefully slit the olive lengthwise down to the pit with a small, sharp knife. Pry the flesh away from the pit; if the flesh sticks to the pit, carefully cut it away.

OREGANO
Aromatic, pungent and spicy Mediterranean herb—also known as wild marjoram—used fresh or dried as a seasoning for all kinds of savory dishes. Especially popular when used in combination with tomatoes and other vegetables.

PANCETTA
Italian-style unsmoked bacon cured with salt and pepper. May be sold flat or rolled into a large sausage shape. Available in Italian delicatessens and specialty-food stores.

ORANGE SEGMENTS
Some recipes call for segments, or sections, of oranges and other citrus fruits, free of pith and membranes.

To section a citrus fruit, first use a small, sharp knife to cut a thick slice off its bottom and top, exposing the fruit beneath the peel. Then, steadying the fruit on a work surface, thickly slice off the peel in strips, cutting off the white pith with it.

Hold the peeled fruit in one hand over a bowl to catch the juices. Using the same knife, carefully cut on each side of the membrane to free each section, letting the sections drop into the bowl as they are cut.

PAPRIKA
Powdered spice derived from the dried paprika pepper; popular in several European cuisines and available in sweet, mild and hot forms. Hungarian paprika is the best, but Spanish paprika, which is mild, may also be used.

PEPPER
Pepper, the most common of all savory spices, is best purchased as whole peppercorns, to be ground in a pepper mill as needed, or coarsely crushed or cracked using a mortar and pestle or the flat side of a heavy knife. Pungent black peppercorns derive from slightly underripe pepper berries, whose hulls oxidize as they dry. Milder white peppercorns come from fully ripened berries, with the black husks removed before drying.

PROSCIUTTO
Italian-style raw ham, a specialty of Parma, cured by dry-salting for 1 month, followed by air-drying in cool curing sheds for half a year or longer.

RED PEPPER FLAKES
Coarsely ground flakes of dried red chilies, including seeds, which add moderately hot flavor to the foods they season.

RICE
Among the many varieties of rice grown, milled and cooked around the world, among the most popular are Arborio, an Italian variety whose short, round grains, high in starch content, create a creamy, saucelike consistency during cooking; and long-grain white rice, whose long, slender grains steam to a light, fluffy consistency. Long-grain rice and other steamed varieties may be subtly seasoned and colored with **saffron** as a colorful, aromatic side dish for fish.

PARSLEY
This common fresh herb is available in two varieties, the more popular curly-leaf type and a flat-leaf type. The latter, also known as Italian parsley, is preferred in some recipes for its more pronounced flavor.

Chopping Parsley
Wash the parsley under cold running water and thoroughly shake dry. Holding the stems together, gather up the leaves into a tight, compact bunch. With a chef's knife, carefully cut across the bunch to chop the leaves coarsely. Discard the stems.

For more finely chopped parsley, gather the coarsely chopped leaves together. Steadying the top of the knife blade with one hand, chop the parsley, rocking the blade and moving it back and forth in an arc until the desired fineness is achieved.

SAFFRON

Intensely aromatic spice, golden orange in color, made from the dried stigmas of a species of crocus; used to perfume and color many classic Mediterranean and East Indian dishes. Sold either as threads—the dried stigmas—or in powdered form. Look for products labeled pure saffron. To best extract their flavor and color, saffron threads should be steeped in liquid before using.

SAKE

Though commonly thought of as Japanese rice wine, this aromatic, dry, clear, 30-proof liquid is actually brewed like beer. As with both wine and beer, it may be sipped with a meal or used as a cooking liquid.

SALT, KOSHER

Coarse-grained salt with no additives and a less salty taste than table salt. Coarse sea salt is an acceptable substitute.

SOY SAUCE

Asian seasoning and condiment made from soybeans, salt, water and usually wheat or another grain. Seek out good-quality imported soy sauces; Chinese brands tend to be markedly saltier than Japanese.

SWISS CHARD

Also known as chard or silverbeet, a leafy, dark green vegetable with thick, crisp white or red stems and ribs. The green part, often trimmed from the stems and ribs, may be cooked like spinach, and has a somewhat milder flavor.

TAHINI

Smooth, rich paste ground from sesame seeds and used in Middle Eastern cooking to enrich the flavor and texture of both savory and sweet dishes. Jars and cans of tahini may be found in ethnic markets and well-stocked food stores.

TARRAGON

Fragrant, distinctively sweet herb (below) used fresh or dried as a seasoning for seafood, chicken, light meats, eggs and vegetables.

THYME

Fragrant, clean-tasting, small-leaved herb popular fresh or dried as a seasoning for seafood, poultry, light meats and vegetables.

TURMERIC

Pungent, earthy-flavored ground spice that, like **saffron**, adds a vibrant yellow color to any dish.

VINEGARS

Literally "sour" wine, vinegar results when certain strains of yeast cause wine—or some other alcoholic liquid such as apple cider or Japanese rice wine—to ferment for a second time, turning it acidic. The best-quality wine vinegars begin with good-quality wine. Red wine vinegar, like the wine from which it is made, has a more robust flavor than vinegar produced from white wine. Balsamic vinegar, a specialty of Modena, Italy, is a vinegar made from reduced grape juice and aged for many years. Sherry vinegar has the rich color and savor of the fortified wine from which it is made. White or distilled vinegar, distilled from grain-mash alcohol, is preferred when vinegar's sharpness is desired without any residual taste or color. Flavored vinegars are made by adding herbs such as **tarragon** and **dill** or fruits such as raspberries.

ZEST

Thin, brightly colored, outermost layer of a citrus fruit's peel, containing most of its aromatic essential oils. Zest may be removed using one of two easy methods:

1. Use a simple tool known as a zester, drawing its sharp-edged holes across the fruit's skin to remove the zest in thin strips. Alternatively, use a fine-holed hand-held grater.

2. Holding the edge of a paring knife or vegetable peeler away from you and almost parallel to the fruit's skin, carefully cut off the zest in thin strips, taking care not to remove any white pith with it. Then thinly slice or chop on a cutting board.

TOMATOES

During summer, when tomatoes are in season, use the best sun-ripened tomatoes you can find. At other times of year, plum tomatoes, sometimes called Roma or egg tomatoes, are likely to have the best flavor and texture; for cooking, canned whole plum tomatoes are also good.

Tomatoes, Sun-Dried

When sliced crosswise or halved, then dried in the sun, tomatoes develop an intense, sweet-tart flavor and a pleasantly chewy texture that enhance savory recipes. Available either packed in oil or dry, in specialty-food shops and well-stocked supermarkets.

Tomato Purée

Good-quality canned tomato purées are available in most food markets. To make your own tomato purée, peel and seed the tomatoes, then purée in a blender or a food processor.

To peel fresh tomatoes, first bring a saucepan of water to a boil. Using a small, sharp knife, cut out the core from the stem end of the tomato. Then cut a shallow X in the skin at the tomato's base. Submerge for about 20 seconds in the boiling water, then remove and dip in a bowl of cold water. Starting

at the X, peel the skin from the tomato, using your fingertips and, if necessary, the knife blade.

To seed a tomato, cut it in half crosswise. Squeeze gently to force out the seed sacks.

Index

ACKNOWLEDGMENTS

The publishers would like to thank the following people and organizations for their generous assistance and support in producing this book:
Steve Roby, Jim Wolf, the staff at Square One restaurant, Sharon C. Lott, Stephen W. Griswold, Tara Brown, Ken DellaPenta, the buyers
for Gardener's Eden, and the buyers and store managers for Pottery Barn and Williams-Sonoma stores.

The following kindly lent props for the photography:
Biordi Art Imports, J. Goldsmith Antiques, Fillamento, Fredericksen Hardware, Forrest Jones, Stephanie Greenleigh,
Sue Fisher King, Lorraine & Judson Puckett, Waterford/Wedgwood, Sue White and Chuck Williams.

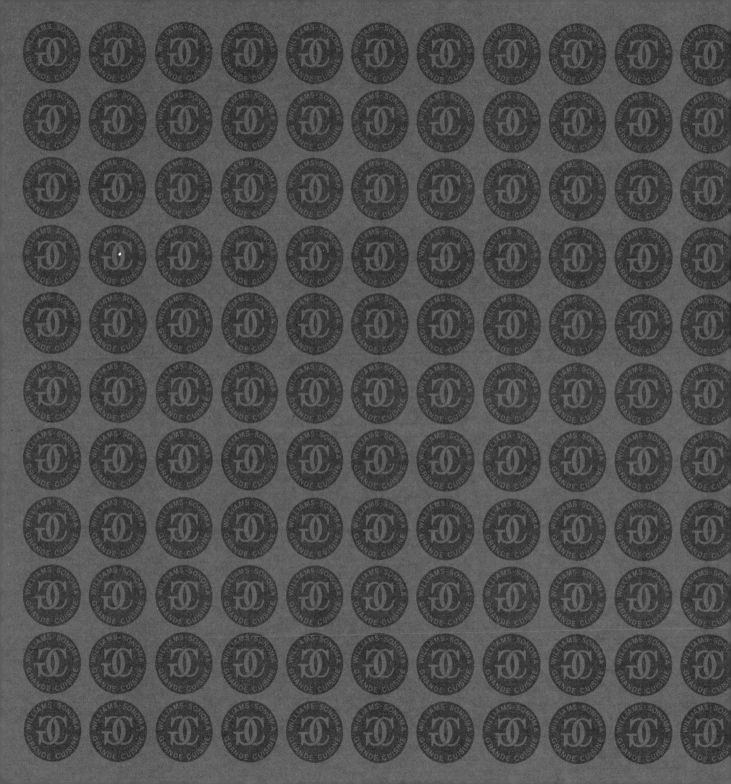